RECOLLECTIONS

OF

MY MILITARY LIFE.

BY

COLONEL LANDMANN,

LATE OF THE CORPS OF ROYAL ENGINEERS,

AUTHOR OF

"ADVENTURES AND RECOLLECTIONS," &c.

IN TWO VOLUMES.

VOL. II.

The Naval & Military Press Ltd

Published by

The Naval & Military Press Ltd
Unit 5 Riverside, Brambleside
Bellbrook Industrial Estate
Uckfield, East Sussex
TN22 1QQ England

Tel: +44 (0)1825 749494

www.naval-military-press.com
www.nmarchive.com

In reprinting in facsimile from the original, any imperfections are inevitably reproduced and the quality may fall short of modern type and cartographic standards.

CONTENTS

OF

THE SECOND VOLUME.

CHAPTER I.

Capture of four Spanish Treasure Ships by a British Squadron, very little superior in strength, on the South Coast of Portugal—General Order 11th June, 1808—We proceed to Ayamonte—I am sent on shore to reconnoitre the enemy—I am feasted—Grand dinner, &c.—I am at the head of the table—I give general satisfaction—I return to the Fleet . 1

CHAPTER II.

Report to the General on board the Windsor Castle—Proceed Westward, and anchor near Cape San Vicente—Go to pay my respects to the General on board the Northumberland—My feather burnt by the explosion of a gun—Captain Hargood—Invites me to be present at a Theatrical performance on board the Northumberland—We all suffer from indigestion, the Captain gives us good advice—Mulcaster's ominous speech—Return to near Cadiz—We land at Cadiz—The former Residence of the Marquis of Solano; an account of his Assassination 21

CHAPTER III.

The Plaza San Antonio, and the company there assembled—The Monks on good terms with the ladies—Baby officers—The Duke of York's regulations to put down the same in England—The General, and some of the troops, including myself, disembark—Hire an empty house—Severe heat—I walk to Xeres and back before six o'clock 37

CHAPTER IV.

Sir George Smith, Charles Fox, Colonel Wittingham—Mr. Frere—The Marquis of the Union—Union Jack and Bartlemy Fair—I accompany General Spencer to dine with General Morla—Ladies Bathing—Review of the British Troops — Captain Preston—Castaños gains the Battle of Baylen—We re-embark and sail to Cape San Vicente—The Chaplain a Drunkard . 55

CHAPTER V.

I proceed to report the conduct of the Chaplain to the Commander-in-Chief—Sir George Smith would not interfere during the absence of Spencer—Captain Cook of the Guards—Expectation of being soon landed—Up anchor and off round Cape San Vicente—Preparations to land—I cut off my long queue—Anchor at Mondego Bay—Swamped in attempting to land in the ship's boat at Figueras—Meet Captain Elphinstone, and resign to him my command—Embark in a boat to go up to Lavaos—Mercer obtains for us an admission to a house—A good trick—Join the Camp—Purchase a pony from Major Viney 72

CHAPTER VI.

Patten's eccentricities—Patten hires a negro servant, and is robbed by him—I am appointed to the Light Brigade — An alarm—Leiria—Lieutenant Festing— Dust—Dinner sent us by the Monks of Alcobaça . 91

CHAPTER VII.

The dust is very inconvenient, and causes sore lips—A cure discovered—Brigadier-General Fane suffered very much—Major Viney wants a swift horse; I lend him the one I bought of him, but he cannot make him go faster than myself—The Bishop of Coimbra— Viva the pretty girls!—We pass through Caldas-da-Reinha—Commence dinner—Firing heard—I bag my dinner—I hasten away towards Obidos—The first life lost in the Peninsular war—I return to camp at Caldas—I reconnoitre the surrounding country— Rumours of Junot's intentions—I return to Caldas, and find Geary's guns—Geary's presentiment—We march and arrive at Obidos—Captain Bradford of the Guards—I ascend the square Moorish tower at the South point of the town to look out with my glass. 113

CHAPTER VIII.

The heights of Columbeira—Sir Arthur Wellesley comes
up into the Tower—I venture to give an opinion, which
is followed—I proceed with Ferguson's Brigade—
Lieutenant-Colonel Lake with the 29th Regiment, his
ominous reply—An Aide-de-camp of the Duke of
York just lands, and deranges the attack intended by
Ferguson—First position of the Artillery whence the
first spherical case shot was fired—The fire is returned with round shot—A Portuguese astonished—
I make a sketch of the ground—Death of the Honourable George Lake—A lady in the action—Bradford's death — The 71st Regiment — Fitzpatrick—
Doctor Gunning 134

CHAPTER IX.

Death of Captain Geary—General Hill's horse wounded—
Captain Elphingstone wounded—Horses loose at night
—Return to the scene of the action—The wounded—
I rescue two men of the 45th Regiment, each having
a broken leg—The blue-bottle-flies—Amputation of
an Irishman's leg by Doctor Gunning—I call on
Captain Elphingstone, badly wounded; his under-jaw
broken 151

CHAPTER X.

Disposing of the dead bodies—Administering the sacrament to the dying—Peasants putting to death those
who had received the sacrament—A devil, not a

CONTENTS. vii

woman—I provide for the safe delivery of the wounded man at the depôt of wounded men—I return to the spot where I had left the army; the whole was gone—I follow, and purchase a horse—Arrive at Lorinha—No supper—I had assumed the command of the Engineers—I now sought for Sir Arthur Wellesley—I go on at the head of the march with Spencer—Sent forward to report on the merits of the position at Vimieiro—I narrowly escape being made prisoner. 170

CHAPTER XI.

My recommendation is adopted—I have a marquee—Reconnoitre the surrounding country — I refuse to give Bathurst a copy of my plan of the ground on which the battle of the 17th was fought—A copy was, nevertheless, published — Robe acquaints me we shall be attacked to-morrow—The action commences—I cut a way for a Brigade of Artillery to pass out of the Park—Great disturbance amongst the ladies—An interesting event—The 50th Regiment—A good laugh at "Who bobs there?" — I serve Brigadier-General Anstruther as A.D.C. — Lieutenant-Colonel Taylor—The Drum-Major—Cavalry turned by Eliott's guns 190

CHAPTER XII.

Column of attack—Severe fire—Robe's noble feelings and devotion—The column advances—The column attempts to deploy into line—Anstruther's address to the 43rd and 50th Regiments—Walker's order and then charge—It was a grand sight—I am ordered to hasten forward and bring back those who had gone on the pursuit—I find it very difficult to halt these troops and make them fall back—I join General Fane—A Rifleman selecting his victim—Capture of a gun—Fane's delight—Two French officers wounded, and in a gravel-pit—General Pillet—General Brénier. 210

CHAPTER XIII.

The French show a line—The space betwixt us—A soldier of the 50th gives me a silver dish—The Dirty Half Hundred becomes the gallant 50th—The field of battle—Fear of poison—Morrison's hat shot through, the same as my own—Shot at by a wounded prisoner—I return the compliment—I find Sir Arthur—Torrens' account of Mulcaster's conduct—Colonel Burn—Lieutenant Price—Sir Harry Burrard—I am introduced by Sir Arthur—Conversation with Sir Harry—Sir Arthur presses Sir Harry to go on—Sir Arthur's conduct thereon—Sir Harry is hungry and wants his dinner—Thomas Robinson's determination to save the gravy—Some plunder of French baggage waggons. 229

CHAPTER XIV.

I refuse a good offer—I write my despatch with an umbrella held over my paper—I deliver my plan of the battle to Sir Harry—Sir Harry made no mention of the Engineers in his despatch, nor did he of the Artillery, which Robe having discovered in time,

CONTENTS. ix

had corrected—The ball falls out of my pistol—More troops arrive—Robe's joy at the arrival of his son, but he was killed at Waterloo—A baggage-waggon plundered — An ammunition-car damaged — Sir H. Dalrymple arrives from Gibraltar, and I go to meet him—The drums beat to arms—The French General Kellerman arrives in the army with a flag of truce—March and bivouac on some wooded hills . . 249

CHAPTER XV.

In making a sketch of the ground occupied by the army, I lose my way—A heavy storm—Alarmed again by the horses—A court-martial—Arrival of more troops —Major Fletcher supersedes me in the command—The whole of the army reviewed . . 266

CHAPTER XVI.

Advance to Torres-Vedras—Procure a cloak—Dine with Fane—Wine in a wide dish—Having lost my right to a marquee, I sleep in a church-porch with Fane—Sketch of the ground—The Zizandra—Interesting dialogue stopped in the nick of time—Bivouac at Monte-de-Agraça—Proceed by the Pass of Bucellas San-Antonio-de-Tojal—Sir Arthur retains the command of his troop as a Division—Captain Elphingstone comes to the army to take leave of us—His wound appears quite cured—On passage to England he brings up his three teeth—We are all displeased at being kept out in open air—Lawson and myself ride off into Lisbon, and arrive at the American hotel. 284

CHAPTER XVII.

At the American hotel we meet other officers—We visit a coffee-house—French officers astonished at our appearance—We drink punch together—In attempting to go back to the hotel we lose our way—Sleep on a stone seat in front of the hotel and return to camp—Lieutenant Wells, Royal Engineers, returns to us; his account of being made prisoner—The Duke of Abrantes gives a grand breakfast—Sir Arthur gives Junot a sharp cut—The General Officers subscribe for a piece of plate to be presented to Sir Arthur; and the Field Officers do the same 304

RECOLLECTIONS

OF

MY MILITARY LIFE.

CHAPTER I.

Capture of four Spanish Treasure Ships by a British Squadron, very little superior in strength, on the South Coast of Portugal—General Order 11th June, 1808—We proceed to Ayamonte—I am sent on shore to reconnoitre the enemy—I am feasted—Grand dinner, &c.—I am at the head of the table—I give general satisfaction—I return to the Fleet.

IN making mention of my meeting with some officers of the Spanish navy, who had been in England in 1804 as prisoners of war, and who had been captured on board of the Fama frigate, one of the four galleons pounced upon by order of our Government, just at the moment when they were about to reach their destination (Cadiz), I must here relate what may be still in the remembrance of several persons, though, as I have met with a much greater number who appeared to be totally ignorant on the subject, or had but a vague and very imperfect knowledge of this disgraceful event, I shall take the liberty of reviving the details as I find them recorded in one of the best authorities. Before, however, I proceed to do so, I beg permission to explain that at the time when those four ships, laden with treasure, were captured, no war had been declared between this country and Spain; but, on the contrary, we were enjoying all the conveniences and freedom of intercourse usual during a period of profound peace. It is, therefore, much to be lamented that, since a political necessity had suddenly sprung up, inducing our Government to feel justified in attacking and capturing those vessels, they did not, at the same time, feel the necessity of appointing such an overwhelming force as should have rendered a vigorous defence evidently uncalled-for to maintain the high honour of the service. A single shot prior to striking the colours would have been sufficient to fulfil the obligations of the case, in order to protect them from the reproach of having surrendered without firing a shot. Although, in the following extract, an attempt has been made to show that the number of guns was somewhat in our favour, yet it was far too insignificant, and too imperceptible at the moment of meeting, to crush at one glance every hope of being able to make a successful resistance; and such were the grounds upon which the gallant men, with whom, five years after my first acquaintance with them, I served in their gun-boats, had resolved on doing their best to save their ships and the enormous treasure entrusted to their valour.

Extract from James's Naval History, vol. iii. p. 280 :—

" On the third of October, 1804, the British Squadron sent upon this important service, and which consisted of the fourty-four gun frigate Indefatigable, Captain Graham Moore, eighteen - pounder, thirty - two gun frigate,

Medusa, Captain John Gore, and Amphion, Captain Samuel Sutton, and thirty-eight gun frigate, Lively, Captain Graham Eden Hamond, assembled off Cape Santa-Maria, on the South coast of Portugal, on the fifth, at 6 A.M., that Cape bearing N.E., distant nine leagues, the Medusa made a signal for four large sail, bearing W. by S., the wind at this time being about E.N.E. The Squadron immediately wore, and made sail in chase. At 8 A.M. the strangers, which were the Spanish forty-gun frigate Medea, Rear-Admiral Don José Bustamente, and thirty-four gun frigate, Fama (with broad pendant), Clara, and Mercedes, formed the line of battle a-head in the following order: Fama, Medea, Mercedes, and Clara. At 9h. 5m. A.M. the Medusa placed herself within half-pistol-shot on the weather beam of the Fama. Presently the Indefatigable took a similar station by the side of the Medea, and the Amphion and Lively, as they came up, ranged alongside the Mercedes and Clara; the Amphion judiciously running to leeward of her opponent.

"After ineffectually hailing the Medea to

shorten sail, the Indefatigable fired a shot across her fore-foot, on which the Spanish frigate did as she had been requested. Capt. Moore then sent Lieutenant Thomas Arscott to inform the Spanish commanding officer that his orders were to detain the Squadron, and that it was his wish to execute those orders without bloodshed, but that the Spanish Admiral's determination must be instantly made. The boat not returning as soon as expected, the Indefatigable made a signal for her, and, to enforce it, fired a shot a-head of the Medea. The officer having, at length, returned with an unsatisfactory answer, the Indefatigable, at about 9h. 30m. A.M. fired a second shot a-head of the Medea, and bore down close upon her weather-bow. Immediately the Mercedes fired into the Amphion, and, in a few seconds afterwards, the Medea opened her fire upon the Indefatigable. The latter then made the signal for close battle, and it instantly commenced. At the end of about 9m. the Mercedes blew up alongside of the Amphion with a tremendous explosion.

In a minute or two after, the Fama struck her colours; but, on the Medusa's ceasing her fire, re-hoisted them, and attempted to make off. The Medusa immediately bore up under the Spanish frigate's stern, and poured in a heavy fire, but the Fama continued her course to leeward. Having sustained during 17m. the Indefatigable's heavy broadsides, and finding a new opponent in the Amphion, who had advanced on her starboard quarter, the Medea surrendered. In another 5m. the Clara did the same, and the Lively was left at liberty to aid the Medea in the pursuit of the Fama. At about 45m. past noon, the Lively, being an admirable sailer, got near enough to fire her bow guns at the Fama, and at 1h. 15m. this, the only remaining Spanish frigate, struck to the two British frigates in chase of her.

       Indefatigable - - - - 44 guns.
       Lively - - - - - 38 = 46
       Amphion - - - - - 40
       Medusa - - - - - 40

LOSS OF THE BRITISH.

Lively - - - 2 killed 4 wounded.
Amphion - - 0 ,, 3 ,,
Indefatigable - 0 ,, 0 ,,
Medusa - - 0 ,, 0 ,,

LOSS OF THE SPANIARDS.

Medea - 42 - 2 killed 10 wounded.
Fama - - 11 ,, 50 ,,
Clara - - 7 ,, 20 ,,
Mercedes loss about 239.

"It is, therefore, quite clear that the Indefatigable, and any two of her three consorts, would have been a match, even in time of notorious war, for these four Spanish frigates. As it was, the latter defended themselves with the characteristic bravery of Spaniards, notwithstanding that they could have been in no state of preparation, and that the melancholy loss of one of their number so early in the action increased the odds against them. As regards the ship that blew up, one of the passengers on board the Mercedes was a merchant, named Alvear, with his wife, four grown-up daughters, and five full-grown sons, and thirty thousand pounds, the savings of thirty years; he himself, and one son, having gone on board another ship just before the explosion, he was saved, but all the others perished. The British Government gave him the thirty thousand pounds out of the treasure captured in the other ships."

It is quite needless to make any comment on the above statement, which seems to have been drawn up in the hope of justifying, or of, at least, palliating the reckless course adopted for the unjust seizure of the unfortunate galleons, by which *two hundred and seventy to two hundred and eighty lives* were wantonly sacrificed. Why were not two ships of the line added to the frigates? Why send just four frigates to capture four frigates, no matter about the paltry half-dozen guns more on one side?

The ship that blew up contained all the ladies of the officers retiring home after a long absence from Europe.

11th. In the course of this day, the following general orders were issued, and I copy them here, in order to give the names of the officers of the Royal-Artillery, and their distributions, and also some of the interesting details.

"His Majesty's ship Atlas, off Cadiz,
"G. O. 11th of June, 1808.

"Lieutenant-Colonel Ramsay being arrived, he will assume the command of all the Artillery. Captain Loyd is to act as Adjutant, and Lieutenant Mitchell as Quarter-Master to the Royal Artillery.

"One six-pounder and one light howitzer will be attached to the first brigade, under the charge of Captain F. Smith and Lieutenant Holloway of the Artillery. One six-pounder and one howitzer will be attached to the second brigade, under Captain Morrison and Lieutenant Johnstone. One six-pounder and one howitzer to the 6th Regiment, under Lieutenants Thompson and Leathes; and one six-pounder and one howitzer to the reserve, under Captain Cowley and Lieutenant Festing. The brigade of twelve-pounders will be held in reserve.

"The infantry corps are to be formed two deep. The 1st and 2nd Brigades will form a front line, the former on the right and supported by the reserve, the latter on the left, supported by the 6th Regiment.

"When the troops land, the officers are to take on shore with them, in the first instance, no more baggage than they can carry on their own persons, unless otherwise ordered; the men will land with their knapsacks and great coats neatly folded, canteens filled with water, haversacks, &c.

"A serjeant and private to be left on board each transport in charge of the baggage, and convalescent or weakly men to be selected for this duty.

"The troops must land with sixty rounds of ball-cartridge, and a spare flint per man, perfectly good; and Lieutenant-Colonel Ramsay will cause additional ammunition to be also landed for them.

"The Inspector of Hospitals (Doctor Chapter) will take care that the medical officers are prepared to land with the troops, and with the proper field equipments."

On the following day, orders having been given for preparing to go to sea, and a return of the quantity of provision on board of each ship having been required, I went with it myself to the agent of transports. I there found Captain Preston, from whom I learnt that we were now destined to proceed to Ayamonte, a Spanish frontier town, at the mouth of the Guadiana, with a view of pouncing on a small corps of French troops occupying the Portuguese town called Villa Real, immediately on the opposite side of the river.

Accordingly, we sailed, I believe, on the following day; and having anchored at about four miles from the mouth of the Guadiana, (on the 14th of June) my signal was made to repair on board the Windsor Castle, carrying the Commander-in-Chief.

I was now informed by General Spencer, that he wished me to proceed to Ayamonte, and reconnoitre the position occupied by the enemy at Villa-Real, on the right bank of the Guadiana.

My attention was particularly called to the means which the enemy might have of making his escape, in the event of our landing on the sea-shore, two or three miles to the Westward of the town of Villa-Real, and near a small fort called Monte-Gordo.

A Spanish falucha, it was arranged, should call for me on board my transport after dark, in which I was to embark, and proceed to Ayamonte, *viá* the village of Margarita, seated in a swampy channel Eastward of the direct entrance to the Guadiana.

Having received all my instructions, and having made a hearty dinner, I loaded my pistols, stuck them in my sash, and at nine o'clock I embarked in the falucha, and proceeded towards my destination perfectly unattended, for I did not even take my servant with me.

Soon after daylight on the following morning, we touched at Margarita for half-an-hour, and then proceeded towards Ayamonte, at which place I was received by a vast concourse of people with every demonstration of joy, for my arrival there seems to have been expected; and a Spanish Captain of the Navy, who spoke the English language very perfectly, met me at my landing to escort me, and afford me every information.

Having completed my reconnoissance, and having procured, as I thought, much valuable information, I was conducted at about one o'clock to the town-hall, where a handsome dinner, entirely served on silver, had been prepared. According to the Spanish fashion, I was now placed at the head of the table to do the honours of the feast; and about forty of the public authorities, civil, naval, and military, and some of the principal inhabitants of Ayamonte, sat down to the right and left of me.

This was the first time in my life that I had been called upon to play the first fiddle on so important an occasion. I had never even been present at any meeting bearing the slightest affinity to it; and here I was suddenly called upon single-handed to represent the British nation at a political dinner, at which were assembled the highest personages in the town; and, moreover, I was not there as a guest, but seated at the head of the table as lord of the feast, and expected to do the honours in accordance with the customs and manners of a foreign nation, with whom but ten days before that time we had been at war, and were now on terms of the closest friendship!

To fall so unexpectedly into such a position, it will be readily admitted, was calculated to cause me much perplexity; and although my very imperfect knowledge of the Spanish language, and of Spanish etiquette, might be considered as throwing a considerable degree of impediment to my acquitting myself in a satisfactory manner, I had reason to feel convinced that this very circumstance operated greatly in my favour, since nearly the whole of the company present were just as ignorant of English customs and manners as I was of those of Spain. Moreover, the high good humour and general determination to view everything in its best colours, placed me on such terms with them all, that every word I uttered, and every sentiment I expressed, were received in the most enthusiastic manner; for they were fully persuaded, and very justly so, that I could in no case intend to give offence, but that I cordially participated in their raptures at the termination of a long, and, to them, a ruinous war; and at the prospect of speedily being rescued from the thraldom of a rapacious, sanguinary, and overbearing enemy.

On my proposing to drink to the health and restoration of "*Fernando Septimo* to the arms of the Spanish nation and faithful subjects," the loudest acclamations rent the air, both within the room and in the street, where many thousands of persons had assembled, and to whom my toast had been communicated. The firing of cannon, muskets, and pistols, the smashing of empty bottles, and the cries of "*Vivan los Ingleses!*" (long live the English!), produced such a deafening noise, that during the space of five minutes, at least, it was impossible for any of the persons in the room to obtain a hearing. At length, catching a momentary lull amidst the reiterated vivas, the responding toast was given, " To the health of George the Third, let the grateful Spanish nation drink."

The uproar produced by this toast surpassed anything of the kind I have ever heard; the rows at Covent Garden Theatre, on the occasion of the people's demanding the O.P., or old prices, was nothing to it. The whole company were supplied with tumblers, for wine-glasses are not used in Spain, and they now filled them to the top ready for the signal, when it was proposed, and loudly cheered, that this health of healths should be drunk in three bumpers; and, to carry this novelty into effect, each person was supplied with a separate bottle, upon which the whole of the company proceeded, without much noise, to drink off the three bumpers; and, whilst this was going on, it was suggested by one of the magistrates, who had ascended the table, and stood in the centre of it, that, as the toast then drinking was one towards which they ought to manifest the highest respect, and as they could not mark that sense more strongly than by effectually preventing the same glasses from being ever used for any inferior toasts, he proposed that, as soon as emptied, the glasses should be all reduced to atoms by throwing them against the walls. The uproar was now renewed, and, if possible, augmented, by the destruction of the glasses, which were followed by every bottle that had been emptied.

Observing that Spanish heads could not resist the effects of such drinking as would have severely tried those of Britons, I was anxious to close the feast at this happy period; I, therefore, rose, and having obtained a diminution of the noise, in the fewest words possible, I thanked the company for the splendid entertainment they had honoured me with, and also for the manner in which they had drunk my King's health, to whom, I promised them, I should not fail to communicate the whole of the details of the respect they had shown his Britannic Majesty.

A violent effort was now made to propose and drink to my health, and various other sentiments; but the total want of glasses presented a serious impediment to any further expressions in this way, of the prevailing patriotic feeling, which never had been more unanimous than on this occasion. The same obstruction to any further carousing existed amongst the people in the streets, so that I carried my point with less difficulty. Such was the destruction of glasses that I have no doubt, during some time afterwards, a scarcity of that article in Ayamonte was thus occasioned.

I now begged to be allowed to depart, in order that I might report to the British Commander-in-Chief the result of my visit; and was followed to the place of embarcation by nearly, I should think, the whole population of Ayamonte.

On my moving forward to enter the boat, a general rush was made upon me by this vast concourse of gentlemen and ladies, who advanced with open arms to give me the farewell embrace; and thus, during about twenty minutes, I received the kindest embraces from at least four hundred to five hundred of the multitude; and I should not have got off so cheaply had not the master of the boat declared that unless we started immediately, we should not, during that tide, have a sufficiency of water to pass over the bar, or some shallow channel near the sea.

Upon this, several voices were heard from amidst the crowd, calling out, "*Ha! Padron*," or master, "you say that because you are jealous, and you fear that your mistress, or your wife, will get an embrace from the English officer."

"Whoever thinks so is either drunk or a fool, for we should both of us consider such an embrace an honour; but I did not see her till this moment," replied the Padron; "she shall receive his last embrace before he embarks, and make you all jealous: so come forward, Dolores," as he handed up to me a lady with a great deal of style, and who, in a most coquettish manner, held out her arms and gave me a most hearty embrace (not a kiss, for that is contrary to Spanish manners), amidst shouts of "Bravo! bravo!" and the liveliest sallies of wit.

I now tore myself away, and waving my hat, and bowing in every direction, I jumped into the boat, which as instantaneously pushed off from the shore. The cries of "*Viva!*" from this immense assemblage followed me as long as the boat remained within sight.

It was some time after dark before I reached the fleet, and having succeeded in finding my transport, I did not lose one moment in making a rough sketch of the relative position of the enemy at Villa-Real, and of the Spaniards at Ayamonte, showing, also, the batteries, gun-boat station, &c., the whole of which was necessary to explain my report, and which was strongly in favour of the attack.

CHAPTER II.

Report to the General on board the Windsor Castle—
Proceed Westward, and anchor near Cape San Vicente
—Go to pay my respects to the General on board the
Northumberland—My feather burnt by the explosion
of a gun—Captain Hargood—Iuvites me to be present
at a Theatrical performance on board the Northumberland—We all suffer from indigestion, the Captain gives
us good advice—Mulcaster's ominous speech—Return
to near Cadiz—We land at Cadiz—The late Residence
of the Marquis of Solano; an account of his Assassination.

I NOW went on board of the Windsor Castle, to report to General Spencer, and at the gangway was met by Lieutenant-Colonel Bathurst, who very anxiously said that he did not think the General would agree to make an attack, as he had been informed that the enemy at Villa-Real could escape across the swampy valley and river separating Casto-Marim from Villa-Real.

How the General had procured this information I never could discover afterwards, but I was well convinced of its inaccuracy, and, therefore, felt greatly mortified at missing this opportunity of leading the attack; for I am quite sure it would have terminated in capturing the whole of the enemy, about three thousand or four thousand in number.

I am enabled to take this decided view of the subject, having, since then, passed a whole week at Villa-Real, when I had plenty of spare time to walk over the country, and investigate the accuracy of my information, collected at Ayamonte, in 1808, and which justified the recommendation contained in my report of the seventeenth of June, viz., " that the enemy cannot retreat in that direction, excepting exactly at low water ; and even then it is regarded as a very dangerous attempt by those best acquainted with the bogs and soft grounds. I am, therefore, of opinion that the prospect of success is such as most fully to justify the attack; and I should take the liberty of recommending that while every care be taken to conceal that intention from the enemy, by embarking the troops in the boats during the night, and landing them two miles to the Westward of Villa-Real as soon after low water as possible, it is scarcely probable that any failure can occur."

I found the General had so completely given up the attack, that I abstained from pressing it in any way; he seemed, moreover, to have his mind directed to some other more interesting measure, which time has not disclosed to me.

From this place we sailed away to the Westward, and anchored nearly opposite to the fortress of Sagres, a few miles to the Eastward of Cape San Vicente. On the following morning, at an early hour, some of us got into the boat and landed on this rocky coast. Having scrambled to the top, we visited the wretched village of Figueras, where we procured a few fowls and eggs. The inhabitants had never before conversed with

English subjects, and were exceedingly pleased at our visit, and expressed themselves in very enthusiastic terms at the hope which we held out to them, of very speedily restoring to them the Prince Regent of Portugal, at that time in Brazil.

On returning to the transport, some circumstance, which I do not at present recollect, required that I should pay my respects to the Commander-in-Chief, on board the Northumberland, then lying about two or three miles to the Westward of us; and as I ascended the starboard side of that ship, a gun was fired off as a signal, and my head was so near to its muzzle that my very best feather was burnt to the stump.

The explosion was so violent and so unexpected, that I narrowly escaped being blown away into the sea; but I was completely stupified during several seconds, and remained mechanically clinging to the man ropes. On reaching the deck, Captain Hargood met me at the gangway, expressing the deepest regret at the event, and thundering out vengeance against all whom it might concern. In vain

I begged he would take no further notice of it, but he was overpowered with rage at the carelessness of the officer of the watch, the midshipman, the master's mate, the gunner and his mate, the boatswain, &c.: it was their business and duty to have avoided anything so disgraceful to his Majesty's ship, the Northumberland.

Hargood was a little man, full of pepper and fire, brave as a lion, possessing most excellent qualities, a first-rate naval officer, and had never missed an opportunity of distinguishing himself.

Having eaten a sandwich and drunk a glass of wine in the cabin, I took leave; and Hargood following me to the gangway, invited me to return on the following evening, and bring Captain Morrison with me, to witness a theatrical performance by some of the officers and crew; which I very gladly accepted.

Morrison was well pleased at my having promised he should attend, and our curiosity was excited to a considerable degree at the prospect of such an exhibition on board a ship, where everything seemed to stand in the way of such an amusement, particularly through the want of height between decks, and the total absence of actresses. Accordingly, in order to get on board of the Northumberland at the hour appointed, in our best attire, we dropped into our boat by five o'clock, and, after a tight pull to windward, reached the ship. Our reception was everything we could wish : the Captain on deck, and all due compliments were paid us.

We found on board Sir George Smith and General Spencer, with the whole of his staff, and, after partaking of refreshment in the cabin, the whole company was summoned below, where sufficient and convenient arrangements had been made to provide for the visitors and ship's company.

With much care and ingenuity the back seats had been made as much higher than those in front as the height between decks could permit ; and those in front as low as possible; whilst between these and the stage three rows of closely-packed tars were made to sit on the deck.

The play was the celebrated "John Bull,"

and never was that much-admired piece better performed off the London boards. The part of Lady Caroline Breamer was most admirably sustained by a private soldier in the Royal Marines, and that of Tom Shuffleton was exquisitely performed by a Midshipman, who, I understood, had been a lawyer's clerk, in London; in short, all the other characters, requiring so much theatrical talent, were maintained in a manner reflecting the greatest credit on the individuals, the manager, &c.

On dropping the curtain, the efforts of the audience, by the clapping of hands, shouts of " Bravo! bravissimo!" from the officers, and three times three cheers from the sailors, to express the height of their satisfaction, but very imperfectly recorded their enthusiastic feelings.

Another glass of wine and water, with oranges and sandwiches, in the cabin, and off we started to our transport, where we arrived in safety, not without mistaking two or three other ships for our own; and by one o'clock we were safely moored in Blanket Bay.

After dinner one day, we were speculating

on the probable result of our expedition, for it now began to be tolerably certain that our efforts would be directed against the French in Spain, when I observed that, in my opinion, we were about to commence a more formidable course of operations than we had hitherto pursued; and that I should not be surprised if we even marched for Madrid, before we quitted the Peninsula. To this I added that, most probably, some of us would be killed before the re-embarcation of the troops. Upon which, Lieutenant Mulcaster said he thought that would very probably happen, and added,

"Well, gentlemen, you may be all killed if you please; but I hope I shall escape."

Mulcaster was the only one of those present who was killed; his head was shot off at the siege of Badajoz, in the year 1812.

It was about this time that the officers and many of the soldiers on board began to experience much derangement in the digestive organs, perhaps induced by indulging too freely in fruit. On mentioning this circumstance to our skipper, a very plain, unpretending man, he said, he protected himself from that evil, by constantly wearing a wide and thick flannel belt wound round his body twice, and extending from above the pit of his stomach to over his hips, which, although in a hot climate, it might excite an inconvenient quality of warmth; yet a little observation and reflection would readily prove that this course was justified by local habits. And he called my attention to the invariable practice of the people of the sea-coasts in particular, of every nation bordering on the Mediterranean.

"See," said he, "the Maltese, the Moors of Morocco, of Tengier, of Tatuan, of Algier, of Tunis; see the Egyptians, the Syrians, the Turks, the Greeks, the Sicilians, the Italians, the Genoese, and Spaniards, do they not all of them wear these belts? although not all exactly of the same pattern, or put on exactly in the same way; but they are all of worsted, and procured to keep that part of the body well defended against sudden chills." By using this precaution, which is most efficacious, they seldom suffer as we do from indigestion. The above observations, however, chiefly, if not exclusively, apply to sailors and watermen, of course including the fishermen. I communicated to my brother officers the very rational and useful hints of our worthy Captain; but, I believe, I was the only one who profited by it. I put on the belt, and I had no reason to regret it.

Shortly after this, we again returned to our former anchorage, off the harbour of Cadiz; and many days did not pass over before the much-desired leave was granted, permitting Commanding officers and Adjutants to visit the famed city of Cadiz. With the least possible delay, I was rigged out for the occasion, and Lieutenant-Colonel Ramsay, of the Royal Artillery, and his Adjutant, Captain James Lloyd, having agreed to accompany me, we all jumped into the boat of my transport, together with my two Lieutenants, Mercer and Mulcaster.

It would be impossible to fairly describe the joyful reception we experienced on landing at the sea-gate of Cadiz; all classes of persons seemed to be delighted at seeing us amongst them; and we ourselves were never more pleased.

Amongst the numerous objects of interest which had attracted our earliest attention on this occasion, was the house which had been lately the residence of the Marquis of Solano, Governor of Cadiz; and whose attachment to the French party had been so strongly declared, in a proclamation which his Excellency had published, in the latter part of the month of May, that the whole population of the city had thereupon burst out in rebellion against his authority, and immediately denouncing him a traitor to his country, proceeded to his residence, in order to put him to death. The Governor's house, which I believe was his own property, formed the Western angle of a very handsome range of buildings facing the ramparts, and overlooking the harbour and its Northern shores, and was situated in the ward called *el Bario-de-San-Carlos*.

But a few moments before the arrival of the mob at his house, the Marquis had been apprised of the movement, and of the imminent danger to which his life was exposed; merely leaving him time sufficient to order the massive doors to be closed and well barricaded, and to retire to a secret closet in the upper floor. These doors, generally not very inferior, in point of strength, to the gates of a fortress, together with the strong iron gratings to the windows of the two or three lowest floors, presented some obstacles to the first efforts of the populace, as they attempted to force an entrance. This obstruction was, however, but of short duration, for very speedily, two field-pieces were brought up to within ten or twenty yards of the door, which, being loaded with canister, after a few rounds, aided by a sixteen pounder on the ramparts, which had been turned round, soon opened a passage for the infuriated rabble.

During a considerable time, notwithstanding a most diligent search, the Marquis of Solano could not be found; and a report being circulated by some of his friends that he had escaped out of town, the people were beginning to give up their efforts to discover his place of concealment, when a carpenter, or a mason, entered the house, stating that some years before this period he had been employed to construct a secret closet in the upper floor;

to which he immediately directed his steps, and was followed by many of the most zealous in the patriotic cause. The door was quickly shivered to pieces, when the Marquis, like an enraged tiger, suddenly dashed out from his obscure retreat on his enemies, overthrowing every one that attempted to obstruct his passage ; and thus, without sustaining any injury, he succeeded in reaching the flat roof. Solano was hotly pursued. One man, the boldest of his assailants, sprang upon the Governor, who was not only a very handsome, but was also a very powerful, man, in the prime of life. The struggle was short, and terminated by Solano throwing the man over the parapet wall into the street, a depth of sixty feet at the least ; a second, under the same circumstances, shared the same fate ; a third, with no better success, was shot by the Marquis with a pistol ; and almost at the same instant he plunged a dagger into the heart of a fourth. All this while the pursuers continued their ascent, so that in the short space of a few seconds such an overpowering force had collected around the Governor, that he was finally secured and dragged down into the street. On beholding the captured traitor, the populace shouted and uttered the most deafening cries of hellish satisfaction ; and whilst a number of voices were heard demanding that he should be immediately torn to pieces, others insisted on carrying him off to the glacis, on the outside of the Land-gate, the usual place for public executions of criminals, and there hanging him in due form. The distance to this place was too great to meet the consent of such an impatient assemblage, amongst whom were as many women as men ; and the unfortunate Marquis had not been carried one quarter of the way to the Land-gate, when a man, from behind him, pierced him through the back with a triangular sword blade ; and so effectually was the blow dealt, that the point of the weapon protruded considerably through his breast. Solano, without indicating any sensation of pain, very sternly turned his head towards his rear, and exclaimed, "That must have been the act of an Italian! no Spaniard could be guilty of so much cowardice as to strike me from behind."

This noble sentiment, together with the heroic fortitude he had manifested from the commencement, was, however, of no service to him; for, at the next moment, he was felled to the ground, and received a hundred mortal wounds, which he survived but a few minutes; but during that short interval, the bells of the several churches and convents were heard announcing the hour of vespers, a signal never disregarded by the Spaniards; and notwithstanding the ferocious butchering in which the assassins were engaged, the raised knife was instantly dropped, the victim released from the suffocating grasp, when some of them knelt and recited the short prayer; then every one crossing himself and bowing to those nearest him, they resumed their infernal pursuit, and quickly, and in the most literal sense of the word, cut up the body of the Marquis into thousands of pieces. One woman having been so fortunate as to obtain possession of one entire finger, was endeavouring to carry off the valuable spoil, but she was so hotly beset that she was compelled to share the prize amongst a dozen others equally ambitious of possessing it with herself.

Such were the bitter feelings which the treason of the Marquis of Solano had aroused, and such was the character and temper of the mob.

The Governor's residence was then plundered, and the small quantity of wood expended in the construction of a Cadiz building was reduced to ashes. About two years after this event, the ruins of this house were repaired, and opened as a very good hotel.

CHAPTER III.

The Plaza San Antonio, and the company there assembled—The Monks on good terms with the ladies—Baby officers—The Duke of York's regulations to put down the same in England—The General, and some of the troops, including myself, disembark—Hire an empty house—Severe heat—I walk to Xeres and back before six o'clock.

DEEPLY affected with horror and disgust at the details above recorded, and which a Spanish gentleman, on noticing us gazing on the ruins of the late Governor's property, had obligingly communicated; we turned away, thanking our friend for his kind attention to us, and proceeded along the Alameda, which extends between the sea wall and the handsome range of houses, limiting the city on this side. Having arrived at a long and very straight street, leading away at right angles to the left, which we justly concluded would introduce us to about the centre of the city; we adopted it, and thus by the street called Linares, entered the Plaza San Antonio, soon after mid-day. This Plaza, although quadrangular, is not strictly a square; the length of the sides varying from two hundred and fifty to two hundred and eighty feet. The whole is paved with neatly-jointed stones, leaving a way all round sufficiently wide for carriages, from which the flagged interior is separated by fine orange trees planted in boxes; and marble seats placed alternately at short intervals. Three sides of the Plaza are formed of lofty and very handsome houses; most of them have turrets rising high into the blue sky; almost all of them have tall pillars along the front parapet supporting arms or other ornamental devices; and the windows to the second and third stories are balconied, the iron work painted green, and rendered lively by a few touches here and there of vermilion; forming a happy contrast with the dazzling whiteness of the houses. The fourth side of the Plaza San Antonio is entirely occupied by the inelegant church of San Antonio, the clock of which strikes the hours on a cracked bell, and over the door shows the age of the moon.

We entered this celebrated Plaza, as I have already stated, by the Calle Linares, between twelve and one o'clock; at which time all the nobility and gay people of Cadiz, including the officers of the army and navy, and, in short, all persons holding offices under government were assembled, dressed to a man in embroidered uniforms; those decorated with military orders, wearing the stars and the broad ribbon over the shoulders and outside their coats; white silk stockings, shoes and buckles, the whole surmounted by cocked hats heavily laced, and of the first magnitude. Amongst these lounged a profusion of women of every rank and class in society, very smartly dressed. Some of them had several rows of gold dangling Spanish buttons, placed diagonally from their elbows to their wrists; and in one instance, I observed a lady, possibly of rank, but certainly of fortune, with sixty, if not seventy, of such buttons, each containing a single brilliant, of the value at least of fifty pounds. None of the ladies had any covering on their head beyond a thin lace mantilla; to aid which, during moments when the sun emitted its rays with extra strength, the lady held up a small spangled fan over her forehead; but this they much more frequently and more willingly used, by opening and shutting it in a very graceful and lively manner, whereby they convey their meaning, as they pass in the promenade, with a degree of telegraphic skill quite seducing, and exclusively their own. All of them dressed in black, either satin, silk or bombasin, white stockings, and, generally, white satin shoes.

We should, naturally, from such a description, form an opinion that the assemblage would wear a gloomy aspect; but the coloured gloves with silk half handkerchiefs of the gayest colours, neatly fastened over the bust, gave them an air of the most pleasing liveliness.

Amongst them, at the time to which I refer, when about four thousand monks and friars occupied the rich monasteries of San Juan, near the sea, and land-gates; the Franciscans nearer the Plaza San Antonio; the Capuchins towards the light-house, &c.; these gentry failed not to display in the most public manner their gallantry towards the ladies; and, on a subsequent occasion, when I visited Cadiz, I remember seeing one, a very stout man, of the order of San Francisco, named Tili, with whom I was personally well acquainted, promenading in the midst of the throng of the first gentry in Cadiz, with two highly disreputable females, and laughing and joking with them in a way which I expected would have drawn upon him some heavy censures; but I could not discover that it had been in any manner noticed, either by the ecclesiastical or secular world: and when I quizzed him upon the subject, he replied, with much gravity, "You forget, cavallero, we are privileged persons! we are, moreover, bound to take every opportunity, no matter where or when, to reprove, and endeavour by all the means at our command to rescue such unfortunate persons from following the high road to ruin!"

Amongst the brilliant assemblage of persons here, decorated with grand crosses and commanders of St. Iago, Calatrava, Alcantara, &c., I noticed Admiral Alava, whose forehead retained the scars of a severe wound. He had held a command in the Spanish portion of the combined French and Spanish fleet engaged off Cape Trafalgar with the British, under the gallant Nelson; upon which occasion he was wounded and made prisoner; but, through respect for his rank, age, and wounds, he had been permitted to remain on board of his ship, probably under the usual pledge. His ship was immediately afterwards driven on shore, and the Admiral thus managed his liberty; but about the propriety of his conduct thereon, there were various opinions.

We were all much amused on noticing many little boys of different ages, some as young as five years, dressed in full uniform, as officers of the navy and army. All of them wore their hair powdered and formed in a queue, long coats, short breeches, silk stockings, and shoes with buckles, swords, and enormously large and laced cocked hats. These children in uniform brought to my recollection, that, prior to the appointment of His Royal Highness the Duke of York, as Commander-in-Chief of the army, the purchasing a commission in the army was treated as a mercantile transaction—it was neither more nor less than an investment of so much money to receive a high rate of interest. This abuse was carried so far, that as soon as a man was married, and there was any probability of his lady presenting him a son or a daughter, if he possessed a little interest, he was permitted to purchase a commission for the little coming stranger, on the chance of the same being a son; if not, then the commission was sold, or, as I have heard it asserted, it was held on speculation that the next might be a male child; the pay accruing all the time. Through this abominable system, it frequently happened that at the age of fifteen years, a young gentleman had attained the rank of a field-officer; and these practices no doubt gave rise to the story of the nursemaid exclaiming, "It's nothing, ma'am, but the Major crying for his pap!!!" I remember a little boy, only seven years of age, whom I met with his brother, the late Philip Durnford, of the Royal Artillery, at which time he was the Second Lieutenant of the 64th Regiment.

In Canada, in 1798, I was introduced to Colonel Murray, on half-pay, only about eighteen or nineteen years of age. When the Duke of York was appointed Commander-in-Chief, one of his first orders was, that all officers should join his regiment within six months after being gazetted. This salutary measure, at one sweep, cleared the army of its baby officers; and from that moment, the discipline and efficiency of the British army made a rapid progress, and has gone on steadily advancing in the estimation of the whole of the military world.

From the Plaza San Antonio, we pursued our interesting voyage of discovery; and after some five or six hours' rapid inspection of all we could see in so short a time, we found our way to the Posada, called the Quartro Naciones, in the Calle San Francisco, and having well and cheaply recruited our strength, we returned to our dismal floating mansions.

After having been cooped up on board ship during about two months, with the exception of three days in the gun-boats at the capture of the French fleet under Villeneuve, it was not surprising that I should have been greatly out of practice of walking, and we all actually suffered much fatigue at the close of this day's exercise.

In the course of a few days after this, my signal was made to attend on General Spencer, who informed me that he was about to disembark at Puerto-Santa-Maria, a large town opposite Cadiz, and distant about six miles thence; and that some of the regiments, the 29th, 32nd, 45th, and 50th, with a few pieces of artillery under Captain Francis Smith, were to be disembarked there, having been the longest on board of ship; the General adding, that he desired I should disembark also. I landed accordingly, taking Mercer and Mulcaster with me, and we availed ourselves of this opportunity to get our linen washed.

Our intentions had been to get into ready furnished lodgings, but in this we failed, for no such accommodation could be found; we were, therefore, compelled to hire an empty house, which we took for a month; fortunately, the lady who owned the house, requested to be allowed to occupy the ground-floor with her son.

It will be easily understood that, destitute of every article of furniture, and unable to hire any thing of the sort, we were glad of the loan of the merest trifles, which our hostess in a slight degree supplied; but we had neither chairs, tables, nor bedding of the most humble description.

The weather was intensely hot; and although the brick floors provided but a hard bed, still they were cool. In order, however, to form some kind of hollow on the spot upon which I lay, I placed some of my linen, covering the place I required, but made it rather thin in the middle, on which, with my saddle under my head, instead of a down pillow, I slept and dreamed as well as I could have done on a prince's couch.

We had not been many days on shore, when we experienced all the miseries of a Sirocco, of the severest description; nothing can exceed the distressing sensations it produces. The only relief we could procure from a degree of heat so suffocating, was by shutting up the house as closely as would be practised in very intensely cold weather. The exclusion of the external atmosphere was most desirable; but, notwithstanding every care to that effect, all our food was covered with exceedingly fine sand, which was brought floating in the air, from the Great Desert of Sahara, in Africa. The sand thus carried along, was in such quantity, that, although the sky was beautifully clear over head, towards the horizon a yellowish haze was so thick, as to completely conceal from the sight objects at the distance of three or four miles; and in looking from Santa-Maria towards Cadiz, across an expanse of water about five or six miles in extent, the horizon was totally eclipsed, and the sky thoroughly blended with the nearer objects, by an appearance of fog of a yellow tinge.

On one of these days Lieutenant Mulcaster and myself went out, tired of living so long confined, in the hope of finding a billiard-table; and I shall never forget, that, on passing a corner of a street, round which the wind was driving with great violence, we were obliged to put up our hands to protect our faces from the burning blast, which we compared to the heat radiating from a furnace.

On the fourth day, when I fancied the heat had abated, I took my sketch-book and sallied forth, determined to make a drawing or two of Santa-Maria, if possible. Notwithstanding the scorching heat, I wandered about the immediate vicinity of the town, in hope of finding some advantageous spot whence I should be enabled to take a comprehensive view of the town, yet without success. The country is flat, and very bare of trees. At length, in looking from the Alameda towards the North, I observed a range of hills, which, although very naked, I thought might provide a favourable place, whence I might make a general drawing of Santa-Maria and surrounding country.

Not without much fatigue I reached the summit, by the fine wide high road leading to Madrid; and having been informed by some of the peasantry that I was half way from Santa-Maria to Xeres, or Sherries as we called it, I resolved on walking on the remainder of the distance, and paying a visit to that celebrated town; to this I was the more readily induced, on perceiving that the sandy haze rendered every object so indistinct, that I could not sufficiently make out any details so as to sketch them; this effect was stronger in looking towards Santa-Maria in the South than in the contrary directions.

Having made up my mind, I advanced leisurely, and at the expiration of an hour and a half, I entered the suburbs of Xeres. The clocks were striking one, and the heat intense, so that not a living creature was visible; every house was closely shut up, and I began to entertain some serious anxiety as to the means of gaining information as to the locality of a *posada*, or inn, where I might procure refreshment, of which I was in great need.

At length, I fell on an expedient which relieved me from my difficulty. Up to this moment, I had carried my sword under my arm as is much the practice, but I now let it drag on the pavement. The steel scabbard rattling on the stones as I moved on, made a loud and, I doubt not, a very novel sound in the streets of Xeres, and which the lofty houses echoed famously.

In a very short time I observed several persons peeping from behind the rush blinds covering the outsides of the windows; presently, a barber stepped out of his door, as I was passing it. From this professional gentleman I received great politeness; for he no sooner learnt my desire to find the principal *posada*, than he took up his cloak and hat, and insisted on showing me the way to the door, where he thundered away in good style to rouse the inmates, who were already commencing to enjoy the siesta.

My arrival was, as it may be supposed, quite unexpected; yet, having ordered that the best dinner which could be supplied, should be immediately put on the table, the waiter, who was the only person I had seen, was exceedingly polite; and having brought me a bason of cool water, towels, &c., employed himself in preparing the table. To my great astonishment, by the time I had washed and made myself comparatively comfortable, the soup was on the table, and was followed in succession, one dish at a time, by fourteen or fifteen made dishes, all remarkably good.

I was then served with six plates of fruits of excellent quality. Having finished a bottle of very good sherry wine, which I had profusely diluted with very cool water, I called for a cup of coffee, and inquired how much I had to pay? The waiter put on an air and manner which indicated that I must not feel surprised at the amount, which he began to justify by every expression of the great desire his master had felt to provide the very best dinner in the shortest time possible,

He at length stated that he hoped I should not consider fifteen reals, or about three shillings, an unreasonable charge. The preface had induced me to expect his claim would have amounted to two dollars, or eight or nine shillings; so, not knowing how to expend the dollar which I already held in my hand, I desired the man to bring me a glass of liqueur, when I was immediately supplied with a small bottle, or rather a phial of Rosolio, for which the charge was only one real, about two or three pence. Upon this, I gave the dollar to the waiter, telling him to keep the change (about nine-pence) for himself.

Up to this moment, I had not seen any other living creature than this waiter; but now, the fame of my liberality was spread like wild-fire throughout the house; the master, the mistress, the male and female servants of all ranks and stations, ran out from every corner to bow and return thanks; the mistress of the house, in particular, advanced, with an air of the most profound respect, begging a thousand pardons for having allowed a person of my high rank to want those civilities and proper marks of respect to which I was so fully entitled. Thus, the whole of them followed me to the street, exclaiming with astonishment at my proceeding on foot, and repeating their deep regret at having been unable to procure for me any kind of conveyance, which, on my arrival, I had ordered the waiter to endeavour to hire to carry me back to Santa-Maria.

It was now past three o'clock, and I had nine miles to walk during the hottest part of the day, and that, too, without delay, for I had to be on parade at six o'clock. The heat was intense, and the dark reddish brown dust, as light as volcanic ashes on Vesuvius, almost suffocated me. At a cottage, about half way, at which I rested for ten minutes, to procure a glass of wine and water, I was informed that two men had dropped down dead, through the excessive heat, when at work in the vineyards, on that day; and they expressed the utmost astonishment at my having been able to resist the scorching rays of the sun. I, nevertheless, arrived at Santa-Maria in time to change my dress, and be on parade at six o'clock.

No one would believe it possible that I could have walked that day eighteen miles after eleven o'clock. On my return, I found my thermometer where I had left it in the court-yard, overshaded with shrubs, amidst which played a fountain; it then indicated the temperature to be one hundred and eight degrees. After the parade, I took it into a place where it was exposed to the hot blast of the wind, but still in the shade, upon which the quicksilver immediately rose to one hundred and twenty-four degrees.

CHAPTER IV.

Sir George Smith, Charles Fox, Colonel Wittingham—
Mr. Frere—The Marquis of the Union—Union Jack
and Bartlemy Fair—I accompany General Spencer to
dine with General Morla—Ladies Bathing—Review
of the British Troops — Captain Preston—Castaños
gains the Battle of Baylen—We re-embark and sail
to Cape San Vicente—The Chaplain a Drunkard.

ALTHOUGH we formed but few acquaintances amongst the inhabitants of Santa-Maria, we were more successful at Cadiz, which place we frequently visited, and occasionally passed some very pleasant evenings at the houses of these truly most amiable people. Sir George Smith had taken up his quarters at Cadiz, and at his house I constantly met the family of a most excellent fellow, a Spaniard, very fond of bottled porter, whom we denominated Charles Fox, in consequence of his very strong resemblance to that celebrated statesman, but whose real name was Creuz. His two daughters were very handsome and agreeable; and the eldest was some time after this married to Colonel, since then Sir Francis Wittingham. The second daughter Barbara, it was reported, was to have been married to Mr. Bartholomew Frere, brother of the minister, but death robbed him of his intended bride.

Whilst mentioning these parties, I may be excused for relating, that soon after the great change above recorded in the political relations between England and Spain had been effected, his Excellency John Hookham Frere had arrived as British Minister to the Court of Spain, and with him came his brother Bartholomew just named. The enthusiastic feelings excited in Spain in favour of the British nation, in consideration of this most important union against the French interests, were such as to be immediately manifested by the Spanish Government, who created Mr. Frere, Marquis

MY MILITARY LIFE. 57

of the Union. Now, as Mr. Frere, in calling on his brother, always used the abbreviation Bartlemy, instead of Bartholomew, the English wags at Cadiz very soon described the brothers as Union Jack and Bartlemy Fair.

Soon after our arrival at Santa-Maria, General Spencer received an invitation to dine with General Morla of the Artillery, the Spanish Governor of Cadiz; and, as it was always understood that such invitations extend to the officers of the General's Staff, Spencer included me in that number. Accordingly, on the day appointed, General Spencer, his Aide-de-Camp Preston, Brigade-Major Tucker, Lieutenant-Colonel Tucker, and Captain Cook of the Guards, Assistant Deputy-Adjutant General and myself, embarked in a falucha to cross the harbour, a distance of about six miles. I do not now remember if Captain, now Lord Hardinge, of the Quarter-Master General's department, went with us.

General Morla occupied a part of the large house at the Western extremity of the Alameda, near the church of Del-Carmen, usually described as the Engineers' quarters. Several officers and persons of rank were there, and we received every mark of respect and civility that could be expected. I shall not attempt any description of the dinner; it was quite Spanish; and to do honour to the English, several bottles of porter were placed on the table with the dessert. The whole of the ceremony, including the coffee and liqueurs, which commenced at soon after two o'clock, was over, and we were in the street by four.

Morla was a man of fifty years of age, about five feet ten inches high, rather fleshy, of a very yellow complexion, and large dark brown eyes, which invariably avoided meeting those of the person with whom he conversed. As we proceeded along the Alameda, talking over the novelty of a Spanish entertainment, General Spencer turned to me, on whose left I was, and said,

"Well, Captain Landmann, what do you think of General Morla?"

"Why, sir," replied I, "I think he is a precious scoundrel."

"Upon my word, sir, you have not attempted

to disguise your opinion; that is a very bold assertion," drily rejoined the General.

"If I be wrong, sir, in my judgment of that man's character, I will admit I have been grossly deceived, and have profited but little by my studying Lavater," was my remark; after which the subject dropped.

I was, nevertheless, perfectly correct; and my opinion of the man was fully confirmed by his treacherous surrender of Madrid to the French troops a year or two afterwards, and by deserting his sovereign's cause, and placing himself in the ranks of the enemy.

On our way back to the sea-gate, in order to recross the harbour, having plenty of time at our disposal, we did not proceed by the shortest line of streets, but were attracted right and left by many objects of interest. We thus visited one of the principal ice-houses in Cadiz, situated in the street called Linares, and thence returned to the ramparts, which we followed to the sea-gate, where again we hired a falucha for three dollars, the usual price, and proceeded towards Puerto Santa-Maria. The evening was beautifully clear, the sea breeze refreshing after the oppressive heat of a sultry July day, which threw me into a pensive, and, perhaps, somewhat melancholy mood.

"How very charming this is, how sweetly delightful, how sublime is all this splendid scenery, everything seems to combine to render this evening truly enchanting; yet, how soon must it pass away, and time will roll on and on, and leave nothing but the impression of an agreeable dream!"

These, and such as these, were my flitting thoughts, as the top only of the lofty and sharp pointed sail was barely filled with the elevated breeze, whilst the surface of the sea remained unrippled.

My cigar, which I had lighted soon after quitting the mole, was still hanging betwixt my fingers, but my attention had been elsewhere directed, and the fire had long since been extinct. When about midway, the sun descended below the horizon with a degree of splendour I have never since then witnessed; but the paintings of Claude Lorraine have frequently revived in brilliant colours the recollections of this magnificent picture. With the departing light the lofty breeze died away completely, so that it became necessary to put out our oars; and in a short time we reached the bar at the entrance of the river, leading to Santa-Maria. At that moment the rowing was suspended, during the recital of a short thanksgiving addressed to the Creator of all things, for having permitted us to cross the harbour in safety; and, following the example of the watermen, we remained uncovered during the ceremony; after which the *Padron* solicited a trifle from each of us, as he presented an alms-box, into which every one dropped his pence, but I did not understand for whose benefit, or for what particular purpose; probably, however, it was to pay for masses.

On approaching the town of Santa-Maria, dusk had already made much progress; when towards our left, or Western shore, we observed from eighty to one hundred women bathing in a cluster, and only waist-deep in the water, all screaming and making as much noise as they were able; and as we passed within ten yards of them, they abused us in the most perfect Billingsgate style, and endeavoured to splash us with water.

These were the ladies of Santa-Maria. I rigidly intend to be understood the *ladies* of the first circles. They were perfectly naked, and impudent in the extreme. I was afterwards informed that they cared not what they did nor what they said under these circumstances, for they relied on the dusk of the evening and the alteration in their appearance, when divested of clothing, to pass unknown.

Two of these ladies, who had been nearer to us than the rest, I immediately recognized, chiefly through the colour of their hair, which was a light brown, the only girls in Santa-Maria that I had seen with hair of that colour. I met those ladies at a party the same evening, and I taxed them with having seen them in the water; but they, of course, denied it stiffly, assuring me that they had been to Xeres, and had only just returned.

On the following day the whole of the British troops that had been landed at Santa-Maria were drawn-up in reviewing order, opposite to the residence of some Princess of the royal family, and marched past the windows which she occupied, and saluted her, &c., and the General at that moment placed himself at the head of the column with his staff following him. On this occasion Preston was mounted on a light-brown mottled mare; and, by touching her with his finger just behind his saddle, which was not observable by a stranger, he made her kick to his fullest satisfaction, and to the great amusement and delight of all the ladies, who, at the same time that they admired his horsemanship, were struck with his handsome figure and graceful manners. From that moment Preston's fortune with the belles of Santa-Maria was made.

Fortunately for Preston, the day of our departure was not much protracted. On receiving the news of the glorious victory obtained by Castaños, Captain-General of the Province of Andalucia, over the French army at Baylen, under Dupont, the whole of which (25,000 men) were made prisoners on the 20th July, 1808, we lost not a moment, but immediately re-embarked.

It now appeared that we had remained at Cadiz, watching the result of this expected encounter, ready to advance and assist in covering the retreat of the Spaniards, in the event of their being defeated. The successful result of this battle, the most brilliant victory the Spaniards had to boast of during the whole of the Peninsular war, set us at liberty, and we, accordingly, sailed away to Cape St. Vincent, where again we anchored, with the exception of the Royal Artillery, that had joined us from Gibraltar, for these were ordered at this time to return to that garrison.

An event now occurred which seemed to be the *dénouement*, and likely to put an end to a series of annoyances we had experienced, almost uninterruptedly, from the day on which we had sailed from Gibraltar. I have already stated that, in addition to the officers of the Royal Artillery, and of the Royal Engineers, embarked in the ship I was in, the Chaplain of the army, a first-rate dandy, about forty to forty-five years of age, and holding a travelling fellowship in one of the Universities, was ordered to embark in our ship.

Unfortunately for the honour of his patrons and the church, whilst he invariably maintained the character of a gentleman when sober, the moment he became otherwise, his conduct was diametrically the reverse; and, although our sea stock of wines and porter was almost entirely limited to that which I had myself ordered to be shipped at Gibraltar, the reverend gentleman unfortunately never failed to disgrace his cloth by the time when dinner was over, or very soon afterwards.

At first I used every effort in my power, by delicate remonstrances in the morning, with a view to impress him with the propriety, nay, the necessity, of resisting his vicious propensity in the afternoon ; but all this was in vain ; for, although on these occasions he freely joined me in condemning his own conduct, "more particularly reprehensible," said he, "when in the presence of the soldiers on board," and before whom he daily exhibited himself in the disreputable condition of which we all complained, he daily relapsed into a complete state of inebriety. Every day during the commencement of our being at sea, he had fully persuaded me that his resolution was formed and unalterably fixed to abstain from such irregularities; yet every day convinced us that no dependence could be placed in his most solemn declarations on that subject.

The almost insufferable and disgusting inconvenience of having such an individual forced upon us, was very severely felt by every one in the cabin; and it cannot be a matter of surprise that some of our young officers should have played him a great variety of tricks.

It not unfrequently happened that he would order his cot to be hung up by six or seven o'clock in the evening; and, our cabin being small, this almost totally deprived us of the use of it; however, if he had been contented with this, and had gone off to sleep, we should, at least, have derived the advantage of being released during the remainder of the evening from the annoyance of his most insulting and very disgusting language, which he preferred on those occasions. I have known this worthy remain in bed for several hours, quarrelling with every one on board, although no one made any reply.

Sometimes, after he had gone to sleep, acts of retaliation took place; but the tricks played on him were mostly incapable of causing him any permanent inconvenience,

This course did not, however, work any reformation in him, for, the very day following, having had the good fortune to procure a supply of wine and porter from a victualler just arrived from England, that same day he was again in a shameful condition.

As boys, we naturally laughed for a time at such things; but even as boys, we soon became heartily tired of his presence, and the patience of every one on board was completely exhausted. It was soon very evident that, on the first opportunity, our friend would receive severer treatment; and such was the state of our feelings when we cast anchor for the second time under the lee of Cape St. Vincent.

Our first dinner on that occasion was scarcely over, and, indeed, at so early an hour, that none at table had drunk more than two or three glasses of wine, when, upon my making some very common-place observation, I believe, in regard of the wind, our amiable companion bawled out in a coarse and vulgar manner :—

"Sir, there is a gentlemanly way and a blackguard way of saying the same thing."

I must confess I never was more astonished in all my life, as I was at this unlooked-for and most uncalled-for insult. I had, however, made up my mind to treat him with silent contempt, at all times, after the removal of the cloth. I, therefore, made no reply to his extraordinary observation; but Lieutenant Johnson, of the Artillery, who stammered very much, and, as is usual with persons so afflicted when irritated, stammered still more, jumped up, and running round the table to the parson, began by shaking his fist in his face, when, although his under jaw was greatly agitated, and quivered in a convulsive manner, not the least sound came forth during nearly a minute; at length, the violence of his feelings being by this calamity very much increased, some very strong expressions burst out piece-meal, and were, as well as poor Johnson could express himself, followed by violent threats.

I freely admit that, whilst as senior officer

in the ship, I could not personally attack the parson in such a manner, out of respect to the articles of war, which are exceedingly severe on that subject, I was not overwhelmed with grief at the course which I perceived was likely to be followed on this occasion ; so, leaving my champion to pursue such measures as the very composed state of his feelings appeared to have arrived at, I took up my hat with as little delay as was convenient, and proceeded to seek the 'benefit of the sea-breeze on deck.

I had not been there many minutes, when, as I had anticipated, my presence was required in the cabin, whither I repaired immediately, and there was informed that a severe conflict had taken place, in which the clergyman's eyes had suffered greatly, and his nose was discharging the claret in great profusion.

The explanation which I received, left me no option as to the course I was bound to pursue; I, therefore, put under arrest the two Lieutenants of Artillery, Johnson and Festing, for having committed a most important breach of the articles of war. The cabin was, as may be supposed, in great confusion; and the gentleman in the black coat was vomiting forth a general excommunication against every individual in the ship, and that, too, in terms not very different from those used by Doctor Slop, when cursing Obadiah for having been the primitive cause of his cutting his thumb.

I ventured now to express myself somewhat freely and strongly, and certainly I was so far wrong, viewing the condition of one of the parties; upon this he opened such a volley at me, as surpassed every thing I had before experienced.

I now ordered the Chaplain to consider himself under an arrest, to which I regarded him as liable; but this, if possible, augmented his ire, and he treated my authority with extreme contempt, adding, that whilst I was but a Captain, he ranked as a Major, and should take the command and turn me out of the state cabin, to which he alone had the proper right. He now became quite violent and ungovernable, and began to commit acts of destruction, indicating a state bordering on insanity. I, therefore, in my endeavours to prevent, by every means in my power, the continuance of a state of things endangering our personal safety, ordered him to be forcibly dragged out of the cabin and fastened under the companion stairs, where he had not been half an hour, when it became indispensably necessary to **gag** him.

CHAPTER V.

I proceed to report the conduct of the Chaplain to the Commander-in-Chief—Sir George Smith would not interfere during the absence of Spencer—Captain Cook of the Guards—Expectation of being soon landed—Up anchor and off round Cape San Vicente—Preparations to land—I cut off my long queue—Anchor at Mondego Bay—Swamped in attempting to land in the ship's boat at Figueras—Meet Captain Elphinstone, and resign to him my command—Embark in a boat to go up to Lavaos—Mercer obtains for us an admission to a house—A good trick—Join the Camp—Purchase a pony from Major Viney.

The day was now too far advanced to think of hoisting out a boat in order to go to the Commander-in-Chief, whose ship was lying about two miles to windward, and a stiff breeze right a-head was blowing.

On the following morning, our gentleman under the companion stairs was tolerably cool, and would have submitted to any terms in order to prevent the exposure which my official report must occasion ; but we had suffered too much and too long to pass matters off too quietly ; I, therefore, rejected every overture, and pushed off in the ship's boat, to wait on General Spencer. After an hour's hard pulling I reached the ship, and was informed that the General had gone off in the Scout, towards Lisbon ; but that all his staff, excepting Preston, were still on board. I now made my report to Sir George Smith ; upon which he observed that it was a very unpleasant affair for him to meddle with, in the absence of Spencer, since he knew that he took great interest in the welfare of the said individual.

After seriously considering the subject, and having consulted some of the staff, he said he should send Captain Cook (of the Guards and of the Adjutant-General's department) to our ship, in the hope that through his mediation further proceedings might be rendered unnecessary, assuring me at the same time, that he felt convinced I had not resorted to such extremities without superabundant provocation. I strongly urged the necessity of removing the nuisance to some other ship; but this was met, as I had expected, by Sir George observing, that it would be paying a very bad compliment to the officers on board the ship into which he might be transferred, which would be difficult to surmount.

I now returned to my transport, and, very shortly afterwards, Cook made his appearance as usual, dressed in the top of the fashion, with his light-coloured hair curling most advantageously from under his first-rate Bicknell (hatter, corner of Bond Street). Cook was requested to descend into the cabin, where he found the officers under arrest, and the parson under the companion stairs, in a most lamentable condition.

After some time Cook came upon deck, and reported that he had succeeded in adjusting the terms upon which, in his opinion, a reconciliation might be effected; his friend of the black cloth, having agreed that he should apologize for having most unwarrantably provoked the rough handling he had suffered, &c.; and also that he should entreat me to kindly overlook his repeated faults, and that I should release from arrest the two officers who had, through his own impropriety, subjected themselves to be tried by a court-martial, for striking a Chaplain of the army. Cook assuring me that the two officers in question had consented to be satisfied with these terms.

Having now carried this affair just as far as I had intended, and which, I thought, well calculated to cure the Chaplain, for a short time at least, I gave way to Cook's pressing instances, to which I was the more easily persuaded, he having assured me that before the expiration of ten days, we should be landed to the Northward, and there join a larger force, expected to arrive from England; and that General Spencer was gone in that direction, in order to confer with the Commander, Sir Arthur Wellesley.

Thus terminated this affair, which, at one period, threatened some very serious results.

In the course of a few days after this the

signal was made for weighing anchor, and off we started round the Cape, which confirmed Cook's communication as to our future movements. On reaching the above-mentioned Cape, we encountered a strong North-Westerly wind, as is usually the case at that place when the wind is from the East on the Southern coast; and which compelled us to run away to the Westward in search of a fair wind, as the sailors term it; and after a few days we again got within sight of the Portuguese coast, at no great distance from the Rock of Lisbon.

From this moment, our convoying ships of war, after ordering us to spread every sail and hasten to the Northward, themselves pushed on and left the transports to follow them as they could, or as they were best able.

On the next day, Monday, the 8th of August, 1808, while running along to the Northward, at the distance of four or five leagues from the coast, we discovered a large fleet a-head, already at anchor, in Mondego Bay; and which we very soon joined, each picking out the best berth he could find.

The dull sameness of walking up and down the deck, which had been almost our only occupation during a long period, was now instantly exchanged for a scene of the utmost activity.

The cabin floor was immediately covered with trunks, hats, boots, blankets, great coats, saddles and bridles, and every officer calling for his servant to bring back some article he had but one minute before carried out to be dusted or cleaned; the servants, in their zeal to do everything in no time, were tumbling down the companion stairs over one another; upon which, the most expressive epithets were exchanged, without weighing the consequences. Each servant had been honoured by his master with every possible epithet, without producing the slightest effect, or having the least meaning, except that it strongly manifested the greatest impatience to be ready to jump into the first boat that might be sent to take us on shore.

In the midst of all this confusion not a trunk cord could be found—the rascally servants had neglected to take care of them.

From the commencement of this bustle the subject of mutual and general inquiry was, "What do you think I ought to take with me?" "What means of transport shall I be allowed for my baggage?" "Do you think we shall be many days away from the ship?" "How should I know better than yourself?" "I shall take with me no more than I can carry on my back, or my horse if I can get one," was my constant reply. "Shall I be allowed a horse?—shall I be able to procure a saddle?" And to this receiving no answer, he would exclaim, "Well, I shall take my spurs in my pocket at all events, and so be ready under all circumstances, which is the true spirit of a soldier." And laughing out most heartily at the singularity of this application of that military maxim, and which had been very pompously announced—"I shall," said I, "take my night-cap and a spare handkerchief in my breast pocket, and so I also shall be ready under all circumstances." This produced a momentary merriment; and the important military maxim was very frequently afterwards repeated, particularly on any mention being made of spurs.

Having arranged my luggage, so as to render it as secure as I could make it during my absence, I gave it in charge of the Captain, and then took up a position on deck with my spy-glass, and looked out for signals and boats to take us on shore.

It now occurred to me that my long queue might be inconvenient on service; so, after very serious consideration, I resolved on cutting it off, for it was my own natural hair, and it hung most gracefully so low down on my back, that I frequently tied it accidentally under my sash, but in point of thickness it did not exceed that of a tobacco-pipe. There were very few officers in the army who had needed so much fortitude, for almost all, to a man, wore false tails.

From this day the dropping of queues throughout the army may be dated, excepting with the 29th Regiment, of whom I shall hereafter have occasion to say a few words on this subject.

Whilst under sail the sea appeared to be

exceedingly smooth, but the moment the anchor was down, the ship rolled in such a manner that her gunwales almost dipped under water on each side.

We were about a mile or mile and a half from the shore, being amongst the outermost of the fleet.

During some time we observed the debarcation going on from several of the vessels, but not in the ship's boats; they were not deemed safe for taking the beach, where the surf was so high as to be compared to the landing at Madras, by those who had been in India.

The boats used for disembarking the troops, &c., were the country boats, somewhat approximating to the form of a crescent, and well calculated for such a purpose. Having waited, with more or less patience, until midday, and observing that no boats came from the shore towards us, we at length resolved in attempting to land with our light baggage in the ship's boat.

Accordingly, Lieutenants Mercer and Mulcaster, of the Royal Engineers, and myself, got into the ship's boat, and boldly pushed off.

I was steering the boat, and, at first, all went on well enough, although the ground-swell was high; and I feel convinced that we should have landed at Figueras in perfect safety, by watching the opportunities when the swell was not so severe, and by gradually getting round and under the lee of a reef of rocks, which extended from the extreme point of the bay on our left to a very considerable distance, and behind which the sea was comparatively smooth.

Mercer, however, being alarmed at a higher wave than the former, and observing that we were passing within a very few yards of the extreme point of the reef, suddenly seized the tiller, and in an instant turned the broadside of the boat towards the breaking surf; a sea now struck the boat, or rather broke into it, and filled it. Fortunately, we did not capsize, and the next sea heaving us on towards the shore, a vast concourse of the people, who had been watching our movements with great anxiety, rushed into the sea, and seizing the boat by the gunwals on each side, dragged it by main force high and dry on the beach, before the retiring wave had began to carry us back again into the deep water.

Having thus happily escaped drowning, to which the improper interference of Mercer had exposed us, we hastened to the very miserable and poverty-struck village of Figueras, where we partly dried our clothes and the few things we had landed. We also procured some very humble refreshments, after which we crossed the Mondigo river, which at this season was by no means an important stream.

On reaching the South bank we met Captain Elphinstone, of the Royal Engineers, and Major Viney, of the Royal Artillery. To the former I reported my arrival, and that of the two Lieutenants, and he ordered us, without loss of time, to join the army encamped at Lavaos, under the command of Sir Arthur Wellesley. That corps amounted to about ten thousand men, and had landed but a few days before us from England ; these, together with the troops under Spencer, made up a little army of about fourteen thousand men. After a hearty shake of the hand we parted from Elphinstone and Viney, and immediately recrossed the Modigo in search of the commissary. Having found that functionary, he furnished us with a boat to carry us up the river to Lavaos, some miles distant, whence we had but four or five miles to walk in order to reach the camp.

It was nearly dark before we embarked in the boat, with our clothes imperfectly dried; and, although the sky was beautifully clear, with no wind, we suffered very much from cold, which made us regret the absence of our great coats, without which we had imprudently landed. It was past midnight when we arrived at the village called Lavaos, and immediately went in search of shelter, to protect us from the heavy dew during the remainder of the night.

Shivering with cold, we ran about from door to door, entreating to be admitted, but without success; every house appeared to be crammed full with officers or soldiers and luggage. We tried to gain admittance at the house occupied by the Commissary with no better result; for he even refused to allow us to occupy the passage next to the street door, to which our extreme need of some cover had caused us to reduce our claim.

At length Mercer called us aside, saying he had an idea, and by which he was sure we should succeed in getting in somewhere, providing we obeyed his instructions, to which we most readily agreed. Anything that held out a chance of providing us with a shelter from the cold and heavy dew then falling, was too interesting to fail in obtaining our cordial support.

Upon this, without disclosing his happy idea, he desired us to stand back out of sight, and seek the shade, for the moonlight was very bright, and neither come forward nor make the least noise, until he should call us to him.

We did as he desired us, when Mercer began to imitate a female voice in distress, and then sobbing and lamenting in a most pitiable manner—"Oh! that a young woman like me should be left forsaken in a foreign land, to wander about at this time of night. Oh! what would my poor mother say, if she could but see me in this forlorn situation, without shelter, or any one to care a straw about me?"

This farce had not been kept up more than a few minutes, when a window was opened, and a voice in a kind, soothing tone, anxiously inquired, "What is the matter? I will give you shelter; come here; I will come down and open the door in a moment." Mercer now stepped forward, and in grateful terms accepted the kind invitation for himself and his two companions. Captain Douglass, of the Quarter-Master-General's staff, the officer to whom we were under so much obligation, did not retract his offer, and most kindly welcomed us, on opening the door; and being followed by his servant, whom he called up on discovering our wants, he ordered that we might each of us be supplied with a rush mat, and shown into the vacant store-house.

Captain Douglass wished us a good night, and we thanked him, with more sincerity than usual, for the obligation he had so opportunely conferred on us. The servant obeyed his master's orders; we got our mats, a candle, and a pitcher of water; and, although the store was not boarded, it was fortunately not paved, but the floor was hard earth, dry, and level.

On searching about, I found a large empty cask, about the dimension of two pipes; one end was out, and it appeared, by its smell, to have been recently full of wine or spirits.

It now occurred to me that I might convert this cask into a most valuable addition to my comforts; upon which I immediately threw it down on its side, introduced my mat, and lay down in it, having taken the precaution to stuff one of my boots under each side to prevent it from rolling. Mercer and Mulcaster extended their mats, so that their feet reached the side of my cask.

We had not been many minutes thus extended, when I heard Mercer, in a tone of voice affectedly subdued, for his object distinctly was that I should hear his observations, pointing out to Mulcaster my overbearing conduct in thus seizing on the only cask in the store. "Now," said he, "you see the man we have to deal with; whilst our companion at Gibraltar we used to think him a good fellow; observe his conduct when Commandant—observe it well, and judge by it; we shall have a nice time of it I can foresee." All this I understood perfectly; for I knew Mercer well; he meant nothing more than to try my good nature; and all the while he was thus speaking he kept his feet against my cask, rocking it a little, as if it were by accident.

I frequently remonstrated against this annoyance, but he as often answered that he could not help it.

In the midst of this, I very soon found out that the fumes of the wine or spirit, which still floated about the cask, would not fail to make me very unwell, and I had already begun to feel the effects by the sensation of a headache, which annoyed me very. much ; so, making a virtue of necessity, I jumped out, saying, "You seem to make a great affair about this cask; you may take it if you like." I had no sooner dragged out my mat, than Mercer darted in, like a hound into his kennel, and immediately after fell sound asleep.

At five o'clock in the morning, having had a short repose of only three hours, the cart destined to carry to the camp any little baggage we might have brought on shore, such as saddles, bridles, &c., was at the door, when Mercer was with some difficulty aroused; and it was then discovered that he was perfectly drunk, in consequence of having inhaled the fumes left in the cask; and as he was totally unable to walk, or even to stand up, we put him in the cart on the top of the baggage.

In this style we started, Mulcaster and myself walking by the side, alternately laughing at Mercer's punishment, and at the adventure of the preceding night. By soon after six o'clock we arrived in the camp.

Here we met many old friends of the Royal Artillery and of the Royal Engineers, who were all greatly diverted at Mercer's situation, and at the narration of the mode he had adopted to procure us a night's lodging. Mercer was put into a tent, and a few hours' sleep completely recovered him.

The names of the officers of Engineers, as well as I can remember, were Captain Elphinstone, commanding; myself, second; Captain

Patten; Lieutenants Wells, English, Botler, Williams, Mercer, Mulcaster, and Stanway. Those of the Royal Artillery were Lieutenant-Colonel Robe, commanding, Major Viney, Captains Geary, Rainsford, Eliot, Morrison, Lawson; Lieutenants Patten, Adjutant, Festing, Hawker, Johnston, and many others.

Our friends gave us a good breakfast, and we dined with them also at about three o'clock; and, on my happening to mention that I must occupy myself in endeavouring to procure a horse, for I was not yet mounted, Major Viney said he would sell me an excellent pony, which he had bought only a few days before, but having procured a better, he could spare him to oblige me; and that he would do better than no horse. It was by no means difficult to convince me of that simple fact; I, therefore, agreed at once to take him without even looking at him; and, in order to secure such a prize, I handed over fifty Spanish dollars to Viney, the price which he stated he had paid for him, and which he was willing to take for the pony. Viney had praised the pony as a very sure-footed animal; and, although "a rum one to look at, yet he was a good one to go," particularly over rough ground, added Viney, with emphasis..

CHAPTER VI.

Patten's eccentricities—Patten hires a Negro servant, and is robbed by him—I am appointed to the Light Brigade—An alarm—Leiria — Lieutenant Festing—Dust—Dinner sent us by the Monks of Alcobaça.

AFTER dinner, I was standing near the tent in which we had dined, when Patten joined me with another officer, to whom, as I soon discovered, he had just sold the holsters he had brought with him from England. Upon this I could not resist expressing much surprise at his having parted with an article which I regarded as of the first necessity at such a moment; Patten, nevertheless, declared he thought them of no use whatever.

I cannot refrain from mentioning here another very eccentric measure pursued by Patten at this time, and for which he paid rather dearly. The event to which I advert, as well as I can recollect, occurred as follows :

A few days before my arrival, he was walking about the streets of Figueras, when he met a negro in shabby attire, and apparently unemployed. Patten was, however, immediately seduced by his appearance, and turning to a brother officer who was in his company, said :

"I like the look of that fellow, I have no doubt he would make a good servant; those blacks are generally capital good cooks."

Then going up to blacky, and endeavouring to explain his wishes to engage him by signs and gestures, for he could not speak the Portuguese language, and the negro did not understand any other; but after due diligence had been exercised on both sides, blacky understood that massa was anxious to have the benefit of his valuable services. Mungo's character was so bad, and this was so generally known, that he was in a fair way to starve, so he gladly caught at an offer which so immensely surpassed his most daring ambition, and, therefore, at once permitted himself to be seduced away from his profitable occupations at Figueras,—begging by day from door to door, and pilfering in every direction during the night.

It is almost unnecessary to add, that this worthy availed himself of the first opportunity that presented itself on the march to follow a wrong road; and he thus successfully carried off Patten's mule and baggage together, without having given massa a proof of his superior talent in the art of cooking.

By the orderly book which had been brought to me just before dinner, I found myself appointed to the Light Brigade, as was also Lieutenant Stanway of the Royal Engineers. This Brigade was commanded by Brigadier-General the Honourable Henry Fane, and was under orders to march on the following morning at two o'clock.

I lay down in one of the tents for the night, and at the sounding of the bugle next morning, I jumped up and ordered my famous pony to be accoutered with my handsome new

Mameluke saddle, holsters, and ornamented bridle, &c.; then swinging over my left shoulder my spy-glass in a strong leather case, and my haversack containing a few biscuits, &c., over the right shoulder, I mounted, to which my pony made not the slightest resistance; as such was the patient temper of this excellent creature, that he never attempted to advance one step until I had fully authorized him to proceed. The Light Brigade had been off more than an hour before I started, yet I felt perfectly satisfied that with my famous pony I should in twenty minutes, or half-an-hour at most, overtake it with the greatest facility. Up to this moment I had not even seen my charger; and although friend Viney had described him as "a rum one to look at," I thought his appearance was of a still less prepossessing character; finding, therefore, that in this part of the description there certainly was no exaggeration, I was justified in expecting that his going qualities probably, in an equal degree, had been underrated. With this conviction on my mind, I almost thought spurs a superfluity, and consequently pressed his flanks gently with the calf of my leg; this had no effect, so the whip appended to my bridle was carefully applied at first, then with somewhat more severity; still my pony advanced no faster than a lazy walk; the slight pricking of one spur had no better result, which induced me to venture on applying both of them rather firmly, which, at length, to my very great joy, threw my *good one to go* into a jog-trot. "Now," thought I, "we shall agree;" but the instant I dropped my legs, for it was a very inconvenient position to be in, with long legs on a small pony, the trot was dropped also. I shall never forget the disappointment I now experienced. To be mounted on such "a rum one to look at," and such a *bad* one to go, was no joke when joining the light division of an army, which must hourly, ay, at every instant, expect to be engaged with the enemy.

I became irritated, and applied, as is usual under such feelings, the spurs without much delicacy, and by keeping them fixed I advanced at a gentle trot for the space of about two miles; but at that period my pony made a full stop, and manifested the strongest symptoms of having a will of his own. At length I dismounted, being unwilling to remain on that spot during an indefinite period, and got on by leading him, almost dragging the bridle out of his mouth, until I overtook the army at about eight o'clock, during a short halt to allow the troops time to take some breakfast.

Having first introduced myself to the General and then Lieutenant Stanway, we proceeded, occasionally halting for an hour to refresh the troops; and the General took one of these opportunities for introducing to us Captain Bringhurst, of the 3rd Dragoon-Guards, his Aide-de-Camp, and Captain Macleane, the Major of Brigade; Captain Geary, of the Royal Artillery, who commanded the guns attached to this brigade, also joined our party.

Towards evening General Fane observed that he thought it time to take some refreshment; and having previously ascertained that neither Stanway nor myself possessed the means of transport, and consequently could have no provision but such as we might have in our haversacks, he kindly invited us to partake of some cold meat, &c., which his servant was engaged in spreading on the side of the road.

After this important halt we again proceeded, and as the evening was closing, between sunset and dark, we were riding very quietly at the head of the brigade, when we were startled on hearing a shot fired at a short distance in our front, and in the next moment about twenty men, the whole of the advanced guard, of the 20th Regiment of Light Dragoons, came galloping at full speed against us, knocking down everything on the road; thus, in an instant, we were all pitched over into the ditch; the General's canteens, baggage, and mules, close behind us, shared the same fate.

Fully persuaded that the enemy was close to us, the General halted the brigade, and rapidly formed it into line across the road; and as quickly as the nearest brigades in our rear could be brought up, they were also formed, in order to meet the enemy, and sustain the attack. The Dragoons who had made this precipitate retreat were immediately examined; when they stated, that they had seen one of the enemy's videttes, and had fired upon him, and without further investigation they thought it their duty to fall back, which they accordingly carried into effect very expeditiously.

A more satisfactory inquiry into this event was evidently indispensable; and General Fane, putting himself with his staff at the head of the advanced guard, which had now been re-formed, proceeded to the spot whence they had fired on the enemy's vidette, and very soon discovered a man sitting on the grass by the side of his horse, and whom, upon further investigation, they ascertained to be a corporal of their own 20th Light Dragoons, whom they had shot through the arm, having mistaken him for an enemy.

On being questioned, this man stated that he had quitted his party for a moment, in order to look over a small bank he had observed at a short distance on theright; and, on returning, the country being quite unenclosed, he rode on, cutting off a bend which the road made, without being noticed by his party, and had fallen in with the road beyond the advanced guard, and there waited till his friends came up. Thus, as soon as the two Dragoons, at a short distance in front, perceived this Corporal, the insufficiency of light preventing them from distinguishing his uniform; and not believing there could be a man belonging to the British army between them and the enemy, they challenged thrice, but so quickly, that the poor fellow had not had time to reply, or, if he did, they took no notice of it; but one of them immediately fired off his carbine at the Corporal, and so shot him in the arm. These two men instantly turned round, and made the precipitate retreat already noticed upon their companions, who, satisfied that the enemy must be close at their heels, also retreated, and caused the greatest disorder amongst the leading division of the light brigade.

This was the first shot fired in the Peninsula during the late memorable war, and will serve to show what a trifle will sometimes cause great confusion in an army, but more particularly during a night march.

It was past ten o'clock before all was investigated, explained, and clearly understood, and the order of the march had been re-established. We then advanced again, and did not halt for the night until past midnight, at a place called Cham-de-Ruaes.

Twenty-two hours as a first day's march, was a severe trial on troops just landed from ship-board; but it was said to be unavoidable, through the want of water.

Although my pony had caused me, at starting, to anticipate that I should have the pleasure of walking at least as many miles as I should find him willing to carry me, that is, about half of the whole day's work; the poor creature, after joining the other horses, proceeded as fast as they did, which was invariably at a walk. I now dismounted; and recommending him to the kind treatment of my servant, after taking the precaution of removing the saddle and bridle, which, from that date, served me as my pillow, to the end of the campaign.

I had no great difficulty in selecting the

spot on which to lie down, for the country was quite open, presenting neither hedges, trees, nor bushes, and was as nearly flat as I could judge in the darkness of the night. I, therefore, crept under a cart-load of hay, and by robbing it of some handsful, which I strewed over me, and stuffed betwixt the spokes of one of the wheels, which was next to the wind, I lay down, covering myself with a small blanket I had used as a saddle-cloth, and thus endeavoured to sleep ; but, notwithstanding all my efforts, the night was so cold, and the ground, or rather the grass, was so wet with dew, that I remained shivering until the bugle announced the hour for morning parade about three o'clock.

Having remained in order of battle until after full day-light (11th of August, 1808), the army moved on cautiously, for we hourly expected to come up with the enemy.

Early in the day we arrived at Leiria, a good town, with an ancient castle, built by Denis, seated on a mound commanding the town, but now in ruins. Here we halted during the 12th and 13th, in order to make a new arrangement, forced upon us by the almost total want of the means of transport. Having no superfluities with the army, it became exceedingly difficult to determine how to reduce our wants; yet something, it was clear, must be left behind. We had no more provision than was indispensable, and without which we could not move; our ammunition was barely sufficient. Upon the most moderate calculation, we could not, therefore, diminish its weight without paralyzing the objects for which we had landed; the only other item was the medical and hospital apparatus, which, although highly important with an army commencing a campaign, it was unavoidably determined must be abandoned, as were also a few of the field-pieces.

During our halt at Leiria, I made a plan of the castle; and, on my return to the camp which was close by it, I found Lieutenant Festing, of the Royal Artillery, who was seeking me, and who was then suffering the utmost state of distress of mind. As soon as he could muster his ideas, which, from the moment of our meeting, appeared to be wandering and rushing through his mind in great confusion, with tears in his eyes, he exclaimed, that Robe (his Commanding officer) had treated him in a most shameful manner; and he then again burst out in a train of invectives, highly expressive of the agonized state of his feelings.

My long and intimate acquaintance with Robe rendered it exceedingly difficult for me to reconcile any act of injustice with my opinion of his principles; I, therefore, was much perplexed at such an accusation; and it was not before I had several times requested some explanation of the cause of so much excitement, that Festing, full of anguish, at length expressed himself in the following terms:

" What do you think Robe has done?— why, he has appointed me to the reserve guns, as if I had done something to merit that disgrace," &c.

Having said thus much, his tears again flowed most freely; but, on seeing me smiling at his supposed grievance, he stared at me with astonishment; upon which, I lost not a moment in wishing him joy of such an appointment, and explained to him that I should have considered that post as one of honour, since, instead of its being doubtful if he would be brought into action in any engagement we might have, which depended on the attack of the enemy, he now would be sure of being so employed, the reserve being held ready, to reinforce and support the point most severely attacked.

The change which now immediately followed in Festing's countenance was rapid ; from the most sorrowful to a state of half incredulity of his good fortune, then to the wildest joy, he leaped about, snapping his fingers, laughing at the folly of his distress, cursing himself as a fool for having fallen into such an error, and proclaiming that Robe was the best fellow in the world. Having, at length, recovered some degree of composure, he gave me a most hearty shake of the hand, thanked me a thousand times for having rescued him from his delusion causing him the utmost anguish of mind ; and ran off to find Robe, in order that he might express his gratitude, for having selected him to fill a post, which but an instant before he had regarded as one of the most degraded in the army.

Soon after two o'clock, on the morning of the 14th, the bugle sounded, and every one was quickly at his post; we thus remained under arms in a cold, foggy, drizzling rain, until broad day-light, when the troops marched off.

The dust from the commencement of our march had been ever inconvenient, and had taken such firm possession of our clothes, being fixed by the heavy dew and misty rains to which we had been exposed, that I recollect General Fane placing his arm by the side of mine as we were riding together, when he observed, there was scarcely any difference between the colour of his red coat and that of mine, which was blue.

It was about the same time, indeed, probably on the same day, that General Fane held out his hand, showing me the back of it, when he exclaimed, "There's a handsome hand to present at a drawing-room," alluding to its being very much sun-burnt; for very few, if any, of the army were seen with gloves.

Some ten years after that period, I happened to meet Sir Henry Fane in Buckingham palace, when attending a drawing-room, and both of us were jammed into the doorway of the first room, at the head of the grand stairs, there waiting our turn to be admitted. Whilst in this position I availed myself of that opportunity to remind the General of his observation to me in Portugal, regarding the sunburnt state of his hands; upon which he laughed in good earnest, and admitted his perfect recollection of the event to which I had called his attention.

At this moment the Countess of A——, Fane, and myself were standing edgewise, and filled the doorway; I was in the middle facing her Ladyship, and Fane had his back against mine, pressing me in a most unmerciful manner; upon which, the Countess, with a long pin, passed her hand under my arm, and exclaiming, "You wicked dog, Fane! what a nuisance you are!" at the same moment thrust the pin up to its head into Fane's back, which caused him to squeak out most lustily, and caused so much sensation, that several of the attendants forced their way up, which brought about a most ridiculous explanation; and as I was the only person in contact with the Countess, I was regarded as the offender, until matters were clearly explained, the Countess fully exonerating me.

The dust was at this period very disagreeable, it was ancle deep, and as light as the best calcined magnesia; and, as the wind was in our backs, we were constantly enveloped in a dense cloud, which not only blinded and suffocated us in a degree quite insupportable, but the greater evil was, that it thus totally obscured our view of the country in our front, so that we might have been attacked without a moment's notice. Occasional halts were, therefore, rendered necessary, in order to reconnoitre the country to the extent of a mile or more. During these delays it was truly amusing to listen to the conversations and remarks made by the soldiers, particularly the Irish, who invariably express themselves in a different manner from others. During one of these halts a peasant passed us in a field, at the side of the road, and was very knock-kneed, upon which, Paddy called to his friend thus: "Melony, I say, my boy, look at dat fellow, hobling along dare; see, he's got one knee made of sugar candy, and de oder goes licking it all de way."

We had not proceeded very far when we observed a French waggon on the right-hand side of the road, which had probably broken down, and had been abandoned by the enemy; we examined this vehicle with intense curiosity, but it contained nothing.

At about one o'clock we arrived at Alcobaça, and proceeded through that small town without stopping a moment, not even to gather strength to ascend the long and steep hill, which commences in the place itself. On our left we passed close by the immense pile of buildings composing the celebrated convent of Alcobaça, and of which I may have occasion to give a description in its proper place. We, the light brigade, took up our position at a mile or thereabouts beyond the top of the hill, in order to protect the remainder of the army, whilst they took up their night's lodging in and about the town; and we deeply re-

MY MILITARY LIFE. 109

gretted that the nature of our position in the army did not permit our accepting an invitation which the whole of the staff of the army had received to dine with the monks of Alcobaça.

Our inability to dine at the convent having been communicated to the Abbot, a messenger was, in consequence, sent to General Fane, with orders to express the deep regret of the whole of that community at being deprived of the General's company; and, at the same time, to inquire for what number of persons the General might wish to be supplied with a dinner, which should be sent to him with the least possible delay from the convent kitchen.

It is necessary I should here state, that the General's orderly was a German, named Schwalbach, a private in the 5th battalion of the 60th Regiment, a Rifle battalion; and in order to augment the importance of his office, he pretended to be conversant with the Portuguese language, but of which he had a very imperfect knowledge. Now, as the General had invited Captain Geary, of the Artillery, and Lieutenant Stanway, of the Engineers, and myself, to dine with him on this occasion, the party, including the General and his staff, would amount to six; he, therefore, directed his orderly, in compliance with the messenger's communication, to state that he should require dinner for that number. Schwalbach was not a man that would miss a good opportunity, such as the present; so mustering up his best Portuguese, he contrived to explain that dinner for six would be sufficient, but added with extraordinary gravity, and in a tone of voice truly German, "Mit wine fur twelf;" which, after many gestures, and more swearing by Schwalbach, the messenger appeared to comprehend; and he immediately departed at the utmost speed of his mule.

In the short space of little more than an hour, eight men, all well mounted, on splendid mules, arrived at the ground occupied by the General and his staff; each of them carrying a large and apparently a heavy basket. With magical expedition the cloth was spread, and covered with innumerable dishes of the most delicate viands, superlatively well cooked, and without any garlic, which, we feared, would have formed a prominent ingredient. The dinner for six would have been sufficient to satiate six times as many; for amongst the variety now placed before us, I observed a roasted turkey, two boiled fowls with rice, two roasted ducks, a ham weighing twenty pounds at least, two tongues, stews, fricasees, ragouts, vegetables in profusion ; and a superb dessert of melons of every sort—grapes, pomegranates, green almonds, peaches, &c. ; and, to the extraordinary delight of, and greatly surpassing his expectations and intentions, Schwalbach now had the gratification of beholding an ammunition box, which served as a sideboard, covered with twenty-four bottles of the most excellent red and white wines, being a general assortment of Colhares, Hock, Champaign, Port, Madeira, Lisbon, &c.

The healths of the King, the monks of Alcobaça, and of Sir Arthur Wellesley, having been drank with great satisfaction, but without noise ; we cautiously, as officers of the light division should always carefully observe, resisted the temptation of drinking other toasts.

The ham, tongues, poultry, and wine, not consumed, were carefully packed in the General's provision baskets; not, however, forgetting to allow our good interpreter, Schwalbach, to have his share in moderation of the good things and wine, which his thorough knowledge of the Portuguese language had procured in such abundance.

MY MILITARY LIFE. 113

CHAPTER VII.

The dust is very inconvenient, and causes sore lips—A cure discovered—Brigadier-General Fane suffered very much—Major Viney wants a swift horse; I lend him the one I bought of him, but he cannot make him go faster than myself—The Bishop of Coimbra—Viva the pretty girls!—We pass through Caldas-da-Reinha—Commence dinner—Firing heard—I bag my dinner—I hasten away towards Obidos—The first life lost in the Peninsular war—I return to camp at Caldas—I reconnoitre the surrounding country—Rumours of Junot's intentions—I return to Caldas, and find Geary's guns—Geary's presentiment—We march and arrive at Obidos—Captain Bradford of the Guards—I ascend the square Moorish tower at the South point of the town to look out with my glass.

On the following morning (the 15th), having

remained under arms from half-past two o'clock till full daylight, as usual, we again advanced; but, instead of the whole of the army moving on one road, we were formed in two columns, one of them following a road much nearer to the sea than the one I was with.

We now again found the dust as thick and suffocating as it had been from the day on which we had commenced the march; but it was somewhat less distressing than on the preceding day, the wind being from the Westward, or from our right, and across our line of march. The sky was, however, cloudless; and in following a route in a direction almost due South, we necessarily had the sun shining constantly in our faces.

This was not only inconvenient, by dazzling our sight, and consequently augmenting the difficulty of examining the country upon which we were advancing; but the dust, by settling on our under-lips, and the constantly scorching rays of the sun, very soon produced a serious degree of inflammation in that tender part. Through these circumstances, almost every individual in the army was, by this time, suffering serious inconvenience; our under-lips being greatly swollen, and generally completely burst open and suppurating; the constant supply of dust and incessant heat materially tended to irritate the sore, and in many cases manifested a disposition to assume a very serious state of disease.

At length, some one suggested the application of the leaf of a shrub, resembling that of a filbert, to the affected part, taking care to keep one edge of the leaf between the lower teeth and the lip, whilst the remainder, by projecting over or lying on the lip, would effectually protect it from the rays of the sun and the dust also, from the moisture of the mouth. The result was most satisfactory; and in the course of a few days, all the sore lips in the army, the number of which amounted to as many as there were mouths, were completely cured.

It is worthy of remark, that every one who had gone through this very painful ordeal was never again attacked in the same manner, although he continued to be exposed to the same causes. The troops that had joined under General Spencer had then been nearly all the summer exposed to the same climate, although it was only at Santa-Maria where we had encountered the dust; and many of us had been some years at Gibraltar, where the dust and heat of the sun were very much the same, yet we all shared alike, all had sore under-lips, all were cured with the leaf, and none of us were again afflicted through a continuance or repetition of the cause.

Brigadier-General Fane was suffering exceedingly from the disease above named, when I well remember observing, that on his giving the word of command *halt*, to the Light Brigade, his under-lip was so parched and so ripe with inflammation, that it actually split in two places, and the blood ran down to his chin in a moment.

Having, at length, arrived on some extensive plains, our column was ordered to form line, I supposed for practice; and whilst this was carrying into effect, and I was in conversation with Captain Geary and Lieutenant Wilkinson, the latter of the corps of Artillery-

Drivers, Major Viney of the Artillery, usually known as Mad Viney, came up to us at a gallop, as I thought, on a very good horse ; yet he demanded, in a hurried and wild manner, if any one would lend him a good fresh horse, one that could carry him with the utmost expedition to Sir Arthur Wellesley, declaring that he was anxious to make a communication to his Excellency of great importance, and which, I think, he said, was about the passing of a brigade of guns over a bridge.

In consideration of the pressing necessity of the case, I immediately offered Viney the use of my very celebrated pony, which but a few days before I had bought of him, under the assurance of his being a good one to go, particularly over rough ground.

The Major's mind was engaged on matters of too much importance to recognise the pony or his superior qualifications for assisting him in the discharge of a duty of the first consequence ; therefore, thanking me for my obliging offer, he threw himself into the saddle, and applied the spurs most liberally ; and during the same time, having mounted his horse without the loss of a moment, I made off to an adjacent rising ground, whence I might best observe the rapidity of my pony's movements, under the exclusively able management of the Major. Alas! in selling me the pony, Viney had irrecoverably lost the charm, for he was now no better able than myself to make him, as formerly, go so delightfully over the roughest ground.

Such an animal for a man in a hurry, and that, too, under such serious circumstances, was past a joke. After exerting every effort to recover his late power over his old friend, he jumped off, declaring he had never been on the back of such a brute in all his life. We all had a hearty laugh at the disappointment which Viney had experienced; he bore it remarkably well, and I regretted having played him the trick. He was, however, soon supplied by some of the Artillery with such a horse as he had required, and he immediately turned my pony loose, and galloped off. I experienced no difficulty in catching the abandoned animal, and I cast Viney's horse loose, as he had treated mine.

MY MILITARY LIFE. 119

Whilst we were still enjoying the laugh at the adventure just related, we were all struck with the appearance of a mounted figure, which, at such a distance as at that moment separated us, it was exceedingly difficult to clearly define who or what he might wish to be supposed. At first it was conjectured that, by the flowing robe and various colours, it must be a female. We then suggested that the figure, still at the distance of two hundred yards at least, must be a Persian, a Turk, or an Algerine, for a sword was now very clearly perceptible. Several amongst us suspected that a troop of players or mountebanks must have joined the army, and that the advancing incognito undoubtedly was the celebrated Doctor Vanclatterbank. Such and many others were the surmises of our increasing circle, for officers were running up from all points of the compass to meet this curiosity, when, to our general astonishment, we discovered that the mysterious personage was the Bishop of Coimbra in full costume, with a handsome sword passed through a military cross-belt, which the reverend prelate had boldly thrown over his shoulder, declaring that he would march at the head of the Portuguese troops, about six thousand in number, and that he would share with them all the fatigues and perils of the campaign now commencing.

The army having resumed its marching order, we proceeded, and at about three o'clock passed through the exceedingly neat town of Caldas-da-Reinha, a place much celebrated on account of its hot mineral springs, and which, amongst numerous other diseases, are said to cure scrofula. At the time when we marched through, there were a great number of elegantly dressed promenaders in a sort of public garden on our left; and as we proceeded through the streets, from every balcony flowers were showered upon us in the greatest profusion, accompanied with an incessant shouting of " *Viva-oz-Ingleses!*" a compliment we had not before received; and then the people also shouted "*Viva Portugal!*" upon which some of the soldiers, in a merry humour, would echo, "That's right, I say, *viva* the Purty Gals!" supposing the Portuguese to have thus attempted to speak English.

The Light Brigade did not halt for a single moment until we had advanced to the distance of a mile or more beyond the town, and there we stopped, intending to make another sumptuous feast on the liberal supplies of the monks of Alcobaça.

The General having sent off towards Obidos five companies of the 5th battalion of the 60th and 95th Regiments, both rifle corps, and a detachment of the 20th Light Dragoons, the whole under the command of Captain Travers of the 95th, we were all invited to the dinner awaiting us at four o'clock.

Just as Bringhurst had begun to dig into the ham, and I was holding out my plate for a slice, the sight of which filled my mouth with moisture, although up to that moment it had been so parched, that I thought I did not contain a single drop of liquid in my whole body, we heard a sharp firing of muskets in the direction of Obidos; upon which General Fane jumped up, called for his horse, and ordered us, with the guns under Geary, and some additional companies of the Riflemen, to advance with him immediately.

Feeling that I should be quite unable to do justice to His Majesty's service unless I speedily obtained some reanimating food, I seized, without remorse of conscience, on the leg of the turkey which had been amputated for me, at the moment when I was holding out my plate for the slice of the best ham in the world, and just also at the never-to-be-forgotten moment when the first musket-shot had been heard ; and so, rolling the turkey's limb in the large and, happily, most un-Vauxhall-like slice of ham which Bringhurst had cut in a very perfect Aide-de-Camp's style, I wrapped up the whole in an old newspaper, and mounted, trusting to my biscuit and canteen of wine, which I had filled on reaching the ground, for the remainder of my dinner. Thus provided, I felt that I was more likely to be envied than pitied.

Not so, however, with my pony, who had only been allowed his water, and was just commencing his barley, when I had been under the painful necessity of giving him a mouthful of bridle to satisfy him instead of dinner. I, therefore, hastily threw the nose-bag with the barley over my holsters, in order that I might secure for him a supper at least.

As we advanced the firing increased, and from time to time was kept up with vigour; but before we arrived at Obidos, about four miles from Caldas, the skirmishing had ceased, and we learnt that the enemy had fired from behind an aqueduct at Obidos, on our advanced guard, quite unexpectedly. This aqueduct crosses a valley extending between a chain of hills on the Eastward and the town of Obidos, which stands upon and occupies the whole of a triangular mount, and is enclosed by a strong and lofty Moorish wall, flanked with square towers, the whole of which are in a very efficient condition.

The French did not attempt to defend the town, but contented themselves with forming behind the aqueduct; and, as the cavalry and riflemen advanced to pass under it, in following the high road, they stepped out from behind the piers of the arches, which till then had concealed them, and fired a general volley, which, to the astonishment of the party, neither killed nor maimed a single man, nor even any of the horses.

From this point they retreated slowly, firing on our men as they followed, and Travers went on advancing a couple of miles or more ; when, observing that the enemy were receiving considerable reinforcements, he thought it prudent to retire.

On entering the suburbs our reception was very unlike that we had experienced at Caldas ; here not a window-shutter was open ; the doors all closed ; not a creature, not even a dog was in the street ; no *vivas !* to greet our arrival ; but here and there half a face was perceptible, attempting to peep out unobserved, in order to ascertain whether the strangers passing were French or English. All joy was absent, and not a bell was rung to welcome our arrival. It was thus very evident that the vicinity of the enemy operated as a powerful restraint.

During the above affair Lieutenant Bunbury, of the 95th Regiment, was killed, having received a musket-shot through the chest, and twenty-seven non-commissioned officers and privates of the 60th and 95th Regiments were wounded. The officer above-named as killed was the first life lost in the Peninsular war. Brigadier-General Fane remained at Obidos during that night, whilst I returned to near Caldas with Geary and his guns.

On the 16th I rode back into Caldas, and in the town met Captain Eliot, of the Artillery, with his brigade of nine-pounders, drawn by grey horses, who, with the main body, was only then coming into town. Eliot and many others were very anxious to learn from me the truth as to the little affair of the preceding evening, the account of which had been magnified into a severe engagement; and the never-ceasing desire on these occasions to render such information as complete and accurate as possible, had dictated all the details, not only of the movements and evolutions, but had even provided a long list of killed, wounded, and missing.

On my laughing at all those particulars, and flatly contradicting them, my good friends were greatly surprised; and I found it no easy matter to persuade them that the whole they had heard on that subject was a mass of fabrication; at length, having related the simple facts, they remained astonished at their own credulity. I now turned my horse's head round, and went on to Obidos.

My first object was to reconnoitre the whole of the surrounding country. Having very quickly inspected the ground on the West, I crossed the valley to the Eastward of the town by following the side of the aqueduct, where there is a good road leading over the hills by some windmills, and in a direction which I suspected might again join, or in some way communicate, with the more direct road to Lisbon, which is by Roliça. Having questioned several of the country people to that effect, they confirmed me in my conjecture, assuring me that this road rejoined the high road to Lisbon, at some distance beyond the tops of the hills of Columbeira, on which the enemy was then posted.

The hills of Columbeira presented a strong front of steep and broken ground, covered with pine trees towards Obidos, and at the distance of about six miles from that place.

On my return into Obidos, I waited on Brigadier-General Fane, and having dined with him, we walked about on the ramparts during some time, whilst I communicated to him all the information I had been enabled to collect during that day. In the course of our rambles along the top of the Moorish walls, and whilst we were looking at the Eastern hills through our telescopes, resting on the Moorish battlements, still very perfect, some of the inhabitants exclaimed that they could perceive the enemy, in their white canvas great-coats, and that they appeared to be in considerable force, moving slowly along the skirt of a wood. At first sight I was convinced that the information was correct, and both the General and his Aide-de-camp were of the same opinion; but, after I had carefully examined the supposed enemy with my famous three-feet telescope, by Watson, I clearly perceived that we had been deceived, for it turned out to be a large herd of goats, mostly white.

In the course of our conversation, the General mentioned that Junot (the Duke of Abrantes) was reported to have said, " he should make the pipe-clay fly out of us in good style as soon as we engaged his troops;" in allusion, no doubt, to the use which the British army almost exclusively makes of that article. And as this and many other brags of the same French officer were daily the subject of conversation in our army, it very naturally excited our inquiries as to the talents and services of our own commander. To these questions the common reply was, that his services had been chiefly performed in India; upon which I heard officers exclaim, "Oh, if Sir Arthur thinks he can beat the French troops as easily as he has been accustomed to conquer the Indians, we shall suffer severely! we shall most probably be all cut to pieces; and so Junot may say with truth that he will make the pipe-clay fly out of us." Under this feeling, many of us, totally ignorant of our commander's military skill, advanced towards the enemy, anxiously looking for some event that might fill them with that implicit confidence so indispensably necessary to the success of an army, and which, before the lapse of one week, Sir Arthur so abundantly established.

As the sun had been during some time below the horizon, the General pressed my departure with some trifling orders to the Artillery, and I proceeded as fast as I could; yet, before I arrived there, it was perfectly night and very dark; and, as I had taken a road which passes more to the Eastward than the one by which I had gone to Obidos, and which passed through a thick pine forest, I lost my way; but, after an hour or two passed in severe anxiety, I found myself suddenly in the midst of the Light Brigade. The guns had been moved from the ground they had occupied on the preceding night, which greatly increased my difficulty in finding Geary; however, after groping about, and making frequent inquiries of the sentinels, I, at length, perceived my old friend the forge-cart of our Artillery brigade. I was exceedingly fatigued, so, without being over-fastidious as to the regularity of the surface, I lay down near the forge-cart, without disturbing anybody. Before I went off to sleep, Lieutenant Wilkinson, of the Artillery-drivers, came in, he having been away on some duty, about which I did not enquire; he, also, was very tired, and immediately after he had handed over his horse to his servant, he rolled himself up in his handsome blue camlet cloak, lined with white, and lay down under the shelter, from the cold wind, of a large furze bush. Wilkinson had not been many minutes in that snug situation when he discovered that his cloak had suffered a signal disgrace, at which he swore bitterly, whilst we were convulsed with laughter at his luck.

The bugle sounded at about two o'clock on the morning of the 17th, when Geary ordered his breakfast to be got ready forthwith, and as we sat on the very wet grass, drinking our cup of tea, and eating a slice of bread and butter, by the light of a small lanthorn, he asked me many questions as to the result of my reconnoissance of the preceding day; and particularly, if I thought we should come to any engagement on that day; to the latter I replied that I was decidedly of opinion, the enemy intended to defend the position which they occupied on the hills of Columbiera, so we should in all probability be on that day engaged; upon this, Geary turned to his ser-

vant, saying, " Thomas, I shall ride my war-
horse to-day." Then, " Thomas, look in the
basket, and find me that piece of cheese I
brought from home." Thomas soon found the
cheese, when Geary, looking at it very earnestly,
said to me, " I brought this cheese from my
little farm in the Isle of Wight, it was made
by my wife's own hands ;" then half to himself, he went on, " what a fool I am to be here !
what have I to do with campaigning? I have
a most amiable wife—five darling fond little
children—£800 a-year, and a nice little farm !
Please Deed and the pigs, if I but live to see
the end of this campaign, you shall never catch
me campaigning again, you may depend upon
it." This was more addressed to himself than
to me, for now turning to me, he said ; " Landmann, I must tell you, that just as I received
the order to hold myself in readiness to come
on this expedition, my resignation was lying
on the table, waiting for the servant to carry
it to the post-office. I was then at home, surrounded by my dear little ones, and had it been
sent but a day or two sooner, I might still have
been there ; but having received the order to

come away, of course I could not think of resigning." After this, he frequently repeated " This shall be my last campaign."

Soon after day-light the army advanced, and by half-past six we arrived at Obidos, where the advance of the army halted to refresh. I availed myself of this opportunity to enter the town, with a view to get some breakfast, and speedily found myself at a chocolate house door near the gate, and on the left-hand side of the principal street.

The house was already quite full, and having no one to whom I could entrust my horse, I looked in at the window, when I soon recognised a brother officer, whom I begged to hand me out a cup of chocolate. After a while he did so, and exactly at the same moment, Captain Bradford, of the Guards, then Military Secretary to Major-General Spencer, came up, and entreated of me to let him have my cup of chocolate, saying he was on his way with orders, which admitted of no delay, and had had nothing to eat that morning; if I refused to let him have it, he must proceed fasting. Accordingly I gave him my chocolate, which was boiling hot, but with plenty of blowing, and frequently passing it from cup to saucer and back, he contrived to swallow it; and on returning me the empty cup, said, "I am so pressed for want of time, that I must beg of you to pay for me; I am sure, if I should be killed to-day, you will not call on my executors for the few vintems it will cost you." I assured him I should not, and he galloped off as fast as his horse could carry him.

Having had the good fortune to obtain a second cup boiling hot, which I despatched as quickly as was practicable, I proceeded to the high Moorish tower at the southern angle of the town, from the top of which I occupied myself in examining the position occupied by the enemy; and with the aid of my telescope, I could distinctly see them moving about, on the brow of the hills of Columbeira, beyond the town of Roliça.

CHAPTER VIII.

The heights of Columbeira—Sir Arthur Wellesley comes up into the Tower—I venture to give an opinion, which is followed—I proceed with Ferguson's Brigade—Lieutenant-Colonel Lake with the 29th Regiment, his ominous reply—An Aide-de-camp of the Duke of York just lands, and deranges the attack intended by Ferguson—First position of the Artillery whence the first spherical case shot was fired—The fire is returned with round shot—A Portuguese astonished—I make a sketch of the ground—Death of the Honourable George Lake—A lady in the action—Bradford's death — The 71st Regiment — Fitzpatrick—Doctor Gunning.

THESE hills extend perpendicularly across the main road leading to Lisbon, and are broken or divided by several deep and very steep ravines, the beds of winter torrents, and which are thickly covered with pine trees, excepting one of them, which is the highest, and upon the most elevated part of which stands a cross.

Whilst I was thus engaged, I suddenly heard the sound of the footsteps of several persons behind me, and also the rattling of steel scabbards, which indicated the presence of staff-officers; then immediately I heard a voice asking hastily, and in a tone of authority, for a glass, and at the same moment I was tapped on the shoulder and desired to make room, for the space was very small, and insufficient for two persons to rest their glasses, so as to observe the enemy at the same time. I now, as required, turned round, and Sir Arthur Wellesley was before me; upon which I presented my telescope to his Excellency.

Sir Arthur took a very careful survey of the country, as far as it was possible from that spot, and particularly examined the position occupied by the enemy; after which I related to him my reconnoissance of the preceding day, principally in regard of the hills to the Eastward, adding, that I fully believed from my own observation, and also from the information

I had obtained, that the road I had there followed up to the two windmills, led to the rear of the enemy's position, round his right flank, and therefore offered a good opportunity for cutting off his retreat; whilst at the same time, a movement by that route would intercept the expected junction of General Loison with Laborde; the former being understood to be on his march from Thomar, or its vicinity, with six thousand men, and the latter occupying the hills of Columbeira in our front.

Sir Arthur Wellesley appeared to be satisfied with my communication, and not displeased at the liberty I had used in making the above suggestion; for he immediately ordered Major-General Ferguson and Brigadier-General Bowes, with their brigades, and the artillery of the Light Brigade, to march by the road I had spoken of to him; and then said to me; "As you have reconnoitred that country, you will go with Ferguson."

I departed accordingly, bounding with joy at my recommendation having been adopted, and in half-a-minute was out of town to place myself by the side of Ferguson, at the head of the only portion of the army, as I fully expected, which had any chance of being that day engaged; for we were to do all before the others could possibly arrive in time to share in the laurels I had planned.

On reaching the great road at the spot where it passes under the aqueduct, the 29th Regiment was at that moment coming up, with Lieutenant-Colonel the Honourable George Lake at their head, the band playing a country dance. Lake was mounted on a complete charger, nearly seventeen hands high, a light brown horse, with a famous long tail, and the Lieutenant-Colonel was dressed in an entirely new suit, even his leathers, boots, hat, feather, epaulettes, sash, &c., being all new; his hair was powdered and queued, his cocked hat placed on his head square to the front; and, in short, Lake, and every officer in the regiment, was dressed and accoutred in the strictest accordance with the King's regulations. I was so struck with the marked distinction between the 29th Regiment and all the others then with the army, that I could not refrain from observing to Lake, " Well,

Colonel, you are dressed as if you were going to be received by the King."

Lake smiled, and replied with a dignified air, "Egad, Sir! if I am killed to-day, I mean to die like a gentleman."

I went on across the valley with Ferguson, sometimes conversing with Geary, and sometimes with Bowes, always in good spirits; for I now regarded my fortune as secured, having directed the movement which Ferguson and Bowes, and many others, thought must terminate in the capture of the whole of Laborde's division before the other portion of the enemy could come up.

We thus continued to advance about four miles by the road, which was sufficiently retired from the edge of the hills to conceal our line of march, no one daring to go to the right on the crest of the range of hills we were on, lest the enemy should see us. On one occasion, with the General's permission, I reconnoitred on foot to the distance of half a mile; with one pistol in my hand and the other in my sash, I crept along amongst the bushes, and looked over into the valley, where I saw our main body considerably in the rear of us, which I hastened back to report to Ferguson.

Just as I had communicated my information, I observed an Aide-de-camp with two epaulettes, the distinction worn by those attached to His Royal Highness the Duke of York only. This officer came up at a hand gallop, with a fine white sheep-skin covering to his saddle, and extending much beyond it, and ordered General Ferguson to descend from the heights, and join the main body in a front attack; adding, that he had ascertained the road we were following would not lead us to turn the right flank of the enemy, as had been misrepresented, but lead away to our left. I was never more vexed in my life, as I was on hearing Colonel Brown's order. Down we all went, by a winding, steep, and almost impassable road for artillery, and so with much unnecessary fatigue joined the central column of attack, near the four windmills, on a sandy plain partly covered with pine and olive trees. The ground gently descended towards the hills occupied by the enemy, and was within cannon-shot range of his field-pieces.

A few months after this, I was so anxious to know the fact as to the course of the road we had followed in part only, that I availed myself of an opportunity that presented itself, on my return from Peniché, for carefully examining into the truth, and thus to determine if I really had misinformed Sir Arthur, when I reported my reconnoissance as above stated; and I had the satisfaction of ascertaining that had we followed that road, it would have led us round the flank of Laborde's position, as I had reported to Sir Arthur; not to the left, as had been asserted by Colonel Brown. I have never ceased to lament the loss of such an opportunity.

Within fifty yards of the above-mentioned four windmills, I found Lieutenant-Colonel Robe, of the Royal Artillery, preparing to open a battery on the enemy, whom we could in many places perceive, notwithstanding the thick pine forest they occupied.

The columns of attack were speedily formed, and ordered to ascend by the deep and almost inaccessible ravines; some of which were so narrow that not more than two or three men could ascend abreast, and they were so steep, that the soldiers were under the necessity of slinging their muskets over their shoulders, in order that they might have the free use of both their hands for catching at the bushes and shrubs to assist them in scrambling up.

During this time Fane's Light Infantry and Riflemen were rapidly driving in the enemy's Voltigeurs over an insulated hill on our left, of a very remarkable form.

The battery being ready to open, Robe, near whom I was standing, turned to me, and asked what I considered the distance to be from our position to the enemy's line, in a rather oblique direction to our left, where the high road was seen winding into one of the ravines, and which appeared to be guarded by a Swiss regiment, with red coats and sky-blue facings. I answered that I thought the distance might be about eight hundred or nine hundred yards; upon which Robe observed, "I think that must be very near the mark;" and added, "I'll try a Shrapnel at them for that range;" he accordingly ordered a fuze to be cut for eight hundred and fifty yards.

I now took out my glass, and having ascertained the exact part of the line at which the gun had been pointed, I went a few yards to the left to clear the smoke, and when the shell was fired, it burst beautifully, at a short distance, before it reached the line, upon which I immediately noticed a great number of the enemy drop on the ground. A second shell was discharged with similar result; when I suggested to Robe not to fire any more on that part of the line, in order that we might judge by the number of killed what number on the whole might have been wounded and killed by the two shells, for we were sure of gaining possession of the ground they then occupied.

The fire was afterwards directed over the heads of the attacking columns, on two four-pounders, planted at the head of a ravine, in which our troops were ascending, and suffering very much from a rapid discharge of cannister. These guns now turned their fire upon us with round shot, and we thus relieved the infantry from the cannister fire.

At a short distance to our left, perhaps twenty yards, I observed a Portuguese peasant, mounted on a miserable shabby-looking pony, and who was gazing with amazement at all that was passing, and, no doubt, thinking himself in perfect security; but the very first shot that was fired from the four-pounders just mentioned buried itself immediately under his horse, throwing up the sand with violence, so that it literally pitched over both horse and man, just as a shell might have done.

We all thought the peasant had been killed; but in a moment we were undeceived, for both man and pony started up on their legs and made off with the utmost speed; the man and horse seeming to race with each other, until we lost sight of them amongst the olive trees in our rear, whither the shouts and jokes of our Artillery-men followed them.

Having no particular occupation, I took out my surveying pocket-compass, and made, in a hasty manner, a rough sketch of the ground we occupied, and as forward in the direction of the enemy as the progress of the action could permit; and it afterwards turned out that this was the only sketch that had been attempted.

The 29th Regiment ascended the hills by the steepest, longest, and most difficult of the five ravines, the one adjoining the Eastern side of the high point on which stood a cross. The musketry fire directed on them was tremendous, and they suffered desperately, sixty men of the Grenadier company having been killed and wounded. Poor Lake was killed at the commencement, near the foot of the heights, whilst riding at the head of his regiment, and his horse was also killed, it would appear, at the same time; for when I saw them they lay very near to each other. Thus died the Honourable George Lake, "like a gentleman," as he had but a few hours before this expressed his desire.

I made an attempt to keep up with this regiment, but I had not gone far into the ravine before I discovered that, in order to follow this route, I must abandon my pony, saddle, bridle, &c., therefore, having no fixed or imperative necessity to doing so, I therefore returned across the newly-ploughed field to the paved high road, which I followed, and went on towards the ground which the Swiss regiments had occupied. I soon discovered that I was proceeding between the Light Infantry and the 71st Regiment, commanded by Lieutenant-Colonel Pack.

I soon overtook a lady, dressed in a nankeen riding-habit, parasol, and straw bonnet, and carrying a rather large rush hand-basket.

The unexpected sight of a respectably-dressed woman in such a situation greatly perplexed me; for the musket-shot were showering about pretty thickly, and making the dust fly on most parts of the road. Moreover, at this place, several men killed, and others mortally wounded, all perfectly stripped, were lying scattered across the road, so that, in order to advance, she was absolutely compelled to step over some of them.

At first I thought that the lady was unconscious of her danger, or was so bewildered at the surrounding confusion, in which she might have been accidentally involved, that she did not know she was then going towards the enemy. I, therefore, could not resist saying to her, *en passant*, that she had much better go back for a short time, as this was a very unfit place for a lady to be in, and was evidently a very dangerous one. Upon this, she drew herself up, and with a very haughty air, and, seemingly, a perfect contempt of the danger of her situation, evidently proceeding from extreme agitation, she replied, " Mind your own affairs, Sir,—I have a husband before me." I obeyed.

I went on, greatly astonished at this novelty, until I found myself near the turning of the road to the right, and at a short distance from the spot which had been lately occupied by the Swiss Regiment, in red uniforms, and upon whom Robe had fired two Shrapnells only. Not far before me I observed Captain Bradford, General Spencer's Military Secretary, and I believe there was another officer with him, when they turned into the ravine, where the road became steeper and over-hung with trees on both sides. I now for a few seconds lost sight of them, and immediately heard a volley fired, about the spot they must then have occupied; and hastening forward, I immediately found Bradford on the ground, and his horse by him killed: but I do not remember what became of the officer who I think was with Bradford. I believe he was Captain (now Lord) Hardinge.

Bradford was naturally of a high florid complexion, his hair inclining to red, young, handsome, always well dressed, highly accomplished, and ever the gentleman. He was now pale as death, suffering excruciating pain; and, holding out his hand to me, said, " For God's sake! do not laugh at me for showing so much suffering at a slight wound in my arm, yet I feel as if I were dying."

I was much surprised at this declaration, for I could easily perceive that a shot had passed through his thigh, and had broken the bone, whence some blood was already oozing out; and immediately below his heart I observed in his coat a round hole, and from under his waistcoat blood was beginning to make its way, over his elastic drab-coloured pantaloons. I afterwards understood that this shot had broken his back-bone. From his manner it was evident he was totally ignorant of the two principal wounds just mentioned, and attributed his sufferings to a third wound in his arm, which, as he had truly stated, was but slight.

The 71st Regiment, Highlanders, coming up at this moment, Bradford was put into a plaid, and, under the charge of a sergeant, was carried off. I had a strong inclination to secure his watch, yet I feared if I took it from him, it would have opened his eyes to his hopeless condition. I, therefore, pointed out to the sergeant that his watch, with a handsome gold chain and seals, was all complete, and that his epaulettes, sash, sword, hat, &c., had not been removed; yet Doctor George Gunning, to whom he was delivered soon afterwards, assured me that Bradford had been plundered of every one of the above-mentioned articles, including his Hessian boots, and contents of his pockets.

Bradford had not been carried off many minutes, when I met Fitzpatrick, of the Ordnance Medical department, and I begged him to run down the hill, and give him such assistance as might be in his power to afford him. Fitzpatrick went off with the utmost dispatch, but soon returned, assuring me that poor Bradford could not live half an hour.

On reaching the depôt for wounded at the village of Columbeira, Gunning hastened to give his assistance, but perceiving the nature of his wounds, he proceeded to occupy his time in attending to such cases as held out a hope that by his immediate attention they might be rescued from the wide jaws of death. Bradford, on perceiving this, begged he would give him something to relieve him from the sensation of fainting; and, being conscious that nothing effectual could be done for him, whilst Gunning was arranging his limbs in a position which might diminish his sufferings, he said, " Well, doctor, if you can do nothing for me, pray give me a little water." His wish was instantly complied with, and in the short space of twenty minutes afterwards he expired without a groan.

Gunning himself related these particulars to

me, some months afterwards, whilst we messed together at Peniche.

I lamented the death of this most amiable young man as sincerely as if he had been my near relative; and, I hardly need to add, I never called on his executors for the ten vintems I had that morning paid for the cup of chocolate, which probably was the last nourishment he ever swallowed.

It is worthy of remark that Bradford had four good horses: one of them was killed at the same time as he himself fell, the three others were immediately taken by some of the staff; and, strange to relate, they were all killed at the battle of Vimieiro, which took place on the following Sunday.

CHAPTER IX.

Death of Captain Geary—General Hill's horse wounded—Captain Elphinstone wounded—Horses loose at night—Return to the scene of the action—The wounded—I rescue two men of the 45th Regiment, each having a broken leg—The blue-bottle-flies—Amputation of an Irishman's leg by Doctor Gunning—I call on Captain Elphinstone, badly wounded; his under-jaw broken.

I HAD not proceeded much further, when I understood from a staff-officer that a brigade of guns was ordered to come up from the valley in front of the position we were attacking. Geary's anxious desire to be engaged, which he had repeatedly mentioned in the course of the morning, induced me to push off, in the hope of bringing him up before the order might be delivered to some other brigade. My pony made better progress down hill than in the contrary direction; and being well acquainted with the spot where I could find Geary, I communicated the order without much loss of time.

Geary was delighted, and instantly gave the words, "Prepare to mount!"—"Mount!" and from a walk to a full trot, then to a gallop, was the work of half a minute. On nearing a small stone bridge over the rivulet of Columbeira, another brigade appeared on our right, dashing along through the deep sands, and evidently racing against Geary's, to obtain possession of the bridge; for on that must depend who should afterwards move on, there being no order for two brigades. Geary himself took possession of the bridge, a few yards only a-head of both the brigades, and thus gained his point; the other brigade, of course, immediately halted.

I shall never forget the exultation so strongly depicted in Geary's countenance as he led his guns over this bridge, and I was quite astonished at my pony, as I found him freely keeping up with the full trot at which the guns advanced. In ten minutes we reached the top of the heights, where the country was quite open and free from trees, and instantly prepared for action.

The Voltigeurs now advanced in the most gallant style to within sixty yards of the guns, and Geary having fired one gun charged with canister, as he pointed the second, said, " I'll be properly into them this"—*time*, he would have added, but he raised his left hand half-way to his head, and fell to the ground perfectly lifeless. A shot had passed through his head, having entered half an inch above his left eyebrow.

Poor Geary was immediately carried off to a cottage at a short distance from the spot. I speedily followed to render him assistance, if such were possible, and found him laid on a large chest. His servant was sitting on the threshold of the house-door, his head resting on his folded hands, which were supported by his knees. He was evidently bursting with inward grief, for as I approached he raised his face, and, on recognizing me, he nearly fainted, but he neither uttered a word nor shed a tear.

I spoke to him with a view to console or cheer him; and although, at first, it appeared to produce a contrary effect, probably it relieved him by causing his tears to flow abundantly, his sobs and moanings were now truly afflicting to me.

This poor fellow's wife, an Irish woman, was within, by the side of my late friend, giving full vent to her unaffected sorrows. I went up to Geary, whom but a few minutes before I had filled with delight on conveying to him the order to advance *to the last step of his life.*

His countenance was in no respect altered, his eyes were closed, no blood was visible to disfigure his face, nothing seemed to ail him, yet he did not answer my anxious inquiry. A deep bloodless hole over his left eyebrow explained his silence.

Whilst I thus gazed on my late lamented friend's remains, every word of our conversation during breakfast that very morning travelled through my mind in a rapid and most painful manner; and I remained unconscious of anything foreign to the awful subject then wholly engrossing my thoughts. But I was speedily roused from a state of mind and course of thinking in which no soldier in action has the power to continue, by the servant's wife, who, in a few minutes after I had entered the cottage, with tears in her eyes, and wringing her hands with great wildness in her looks, came up to the corpse, and taking him by the arm, called out loudly, " Mr. Geary ! Mr. Geary ! Mr. Geary !" each time louder and louder, " will you not spake one word for your dear wife and children !"

This was repeated several times whilst I was there, although I most earnestly entreated her to desist; but her affliction was such, that she took no heed of me, and went on reiterating her efforts to procure a reply; happily, he was unable to hear any appeal on a subject so distressing.

My duty soon called me away; I mounted my pony, and on reaching the line, at about half-past four o'clock P.M., although I had been absent but some twenty minutes. I found that the shot which had robbed me of my friend, was the last, or nearly so, that had been fired, and that the enemy was in full retreat, covered by a strong body of Cavalry, while we had but about a hundred and twenty of the 20th Light Dragoons.

Some time after this, the enemy having totally quitted the field, and the action being terminated, I was conversing with a group of staff-officers on or near the spot where the last efforts of the enemy had been directed on our troops as they began to form line after storming the heights. We were all still mounted, and amongst the number were Major-General Hill (since Lord Hill) and his brother, a Captain, and his Aide-de-Camp. Whilst talking with General Hill, and passing my hand over his horse's mane, I observed that some blood had stained my fingers, which led to a closer examination of the horse's neck, when I discovered he had been shot through and through, the ball having pierced him about two inches below the roots of the mane, and about half-a-yard in front of the holsters. I immediately mentioned my discovery to the

General, who, until then, had remained quite ignorant of the event, and could not call to recollection any movement of his horse at any particular time during the action which he probably made on being so wounded.

At this moment the lady whom I had seen ascending the hill passed close to us, but did not allow us the advantage of a peep at her face, so that, although I may have met her afterwards, I could not recognise her, and she now hastened forwards toward the advanced guard. General Hill inquired who she was, but no one knew her, though several of the staff-officers, forming the group, had seen her, as well as myself, during the morning, exposed to the severest fire which we had that day experienced. Various speculative opinions were put forth as to who she might be; none, however, led to any conclusive result, and we all very soon afterwards separated.

It was not until this period that I became acquainted with the particulars of Captain Elphinstone's wound, although I had been early informed of the event, and had accordingly assumed the command of the Engineers.

I was also informed that he had been carried to the depôt for the wounded. It was now too late to go to him, I therefore sought Sir Arthur Wellesley, and postponed my visiting Elphinstone to the morrow.

Having reported to Sir Arthur the wound of Captain Elphinstone, by which event the command of the corps of Royal Engineers had devolved on me, I hastened to the head-quarters of the Artillery and Engineers, and immediately communicated to the officers now under my orders the change that had taken place.

On reaching the park of artillery, I found the officers sitting on the ground, very near the spot where Geary had been killed, and just at the junction of the roads from Lisbon and Lorinhã. Some tea had been made and was soon after distributed, of which I partook, and found it very refreshing. It was then about eight o'clock, when Robe stood up and said, "Now, my boys, we have a sacred duty to perform; the remains of our late dear friend, Geary, must be disposed of." We all immediately rose from the ground, and I discovered a very deep grave which had been made, close to the spot we then occupied; and as the house in which Geary's body rested was very near at hand, in a few minutes the corpse was brought, without procession, to the place which had been prepared for it. The body was rolled in a sheet, and Robe ordered the funeral service to be read, I believe by Lieutenant Patten, the Adjutant to the Artillery; after which the grave was immediately filled up, Robe directing that no mound should be formed, in order that the peasantry should have no indication by which they might disinter the body to rob it of the clothes.

This distressing ceremony being concluded, Robe again addressed us nearly as follows: " Now, my lads, having most affectionately discharged our sacred duty towards our dearly lamented friend, we must remember, soldiers have no time to spare for long grieving; let us therefore drink a glass of grog to his memory, and seek that rest which is necessary for the recruiting of our strength, and preparing us to discharge our duty to-morrow." Accordingly we drank in silence to Geary's memory, and extended ourselves for the night. Here I had to regret I could not find a waggon to cover me from the heavy dew, which every night wetted us nearly as much as a shower of rain ; and as I had no other covering than the small blanket I used by day as a saddle-cloth, I felt most severely the want of a great coat.

There was another very important advantage in getting under a waggon during the night, since in that position we were protected from the danger of being trampled to death, by the number of horses which every night broke away from their pickets or fastenings, and then galloped about the army in droves of twenty or thirty together, keeping the whole of us in a constant state of alarm, and it is very surprising that an evil so great was suffered to be nightly repeated.

Here, during this night in particular, after a severe day's work, we suffered considerably from this annoyance, and I believe few of us procured half an hour's sleep throughout the night.

I well remember that several times the horses came so near the spot where I lay that I jumped up, throwing my arms about and shaking my blanket in their faces, by which means I fancy I saved myself from being trampled upon, but in so doing I endangered the lives of others upon whom I might have driven the horses.

Under these circumstances, I was not much vexed at hearing the sound of the bugle, on the morning of the 18th, at the usual hour. I was wet to the skin by the falling of a heavy mist since midnight. Cold, wet, and shivering, I mounted my nag, and having remained under arms until much after full day-light, it was generally expected that we should not advance that day; and as Robe and others were fully of that opinion, I resolved on riding back to the depôt of wounded, being anxious to pay Elphingstone a visit, in order to assure myself of the exact nature of his wound, and to do him any service which might lie in my power; and also to receive from him any instructions he might be anxious to have observed during the period of his convalescence.

Seeing the importance of the case, I therefore retraced my steps of the preceding day; and having passed through the miserable village of Azambaujeira, soon entered on the steep and ill-paved road descending by the narrow ravine, overshadowed by trees and giant myrtle in full bloom.

The day-light was still very imperfect, caused by some fog, and nothing disturbed the death-like silence which now prevailed, but the sound of my pony's footsteps, as he blundered and stumbled amongst the detached pavement. "What a change in the short space of a few hours," thought I; "yesterday these wooded hills were covered in every direction by thousands of living beings struggling for victory, amidst the roar of cannon and rolling fire of musketry, the sounding of the bugle and occasional bursts of soldiers cheering, as they, in succession, gained the various positions of the enemy! Now, not a bird whispers amongst the bushes!" None had returned, or they were still fearful of venturing abroad.

The rapid and dreadful mutability of human affairs here presented itself in the most vivid colour and unquestionable form.

The morning fog still lay heavily on the plain below, extending towards Obidos, and clung to the pine forest and under-brush, covering the branches and leaves with large drops, which as they ran off and fell, were quickly replaced, resembling a succession of tears, and they seemed to be weeping over the hundreds of the bodies so profusely strewed beneath their shade, and failed not to call to my imagination that thousands would soon be plunged into the deepest affliction on receiving the intelligence of the sacrifice of human life which had taken place on the memorable 17th of August, 1808.

I thus proceeded, musing as I went on, and endeavouring to chase from my thoughts an involuntary disposition to dwell too seriously on the surrounding objects, when a doubtful sound issuing from the woods on my left, caught my ear, and engrossed my whole attention.

I pulled up my pony amidst a number of naked dead bodies, all covered with blood, their faces glittering with gore; and hundreds of blue bottle flies were busily engaged in eating away their eye-lids and drinking in their wounds. One man in particular I noticed, who had three musket-ball wounds, forming a triangle in his breast, was not yet dead, for his limbs occasionally were slightly convulsed. His face, as is always the case with the wounded, was smeared over with blood, inviting swarms of flies that were eating away his lips, and were forcing themselves up his nostrils and ears.

Whilst gazing on these distressing consequences of war, I readily discovered the sounds I had heard were those of suffering beings; I, therefore, no longer hesitated, but turned quickly into the thickets, and following the sounds, after much search and at a considerable distance from the road, I found two privates of the 45th Regiment, both with musket shot through their legs, and, consequently, unable to move from the spot (the bones being broken) where I had found them, and had I not discovered their situation, would have been starved to death or burnt alive, since the under-brush was shortly after this on fire in several places. As they were very much concealed by the under-brush, consisting chiefly of myrtle, growing most luxuriantly to the height of eight to twelve feet, I judged it necessary, in order to facilitate the finding of them, to cut down the brush-wood; I, therefore, made very good use of my sabre, which I had had sharpened before landing, and with which I cleared away a tolerably wide space all round them; and then over their heads, as high as I could reach, I hung up various accoutrements to indicate the spot on which they lay.

From the killed, thickly scattered, I gathered a musket and ammunition for each of them, in order that they might defend themselves from the marauders, and then left them, promising to send a party to carry them to the depôt for the wounded.

Having, with some difficulty, returned to the high road, I reached the small village of Columbeira, where the field hospital was established. I there made many fruitless inquiries after Elphingstone, of the soldiers I met, and was by one of them directed to a larger cottage than the others, although consisting of one floor only.

Here I alighted and hastened to the door, within which, at a distance, I had observed much bustle, but on entering I was instantly shocked at the sight of two surgeons engaged in completing the amputation of a soldier's leg; I started back, saying rather quickly, "I beg pardon;" the patient was seated on a table, holding up with both his hands the stump of his leg under operation, which was below the knee and singing, "God save the King," with the utmost strength of his voice; but on my begging pardon and turning away, he suspended his song, and exclaimed with a strong Irish accent, "Walk in, Sir, no offence at all, Sir." He was a man about thirty years of age, with a fresh complexion and red hair. On turning from the door I had nearly stumbled over two little drummers whom I had not before observed, but I now discovered they were engaged in warming in the sunshine long pieces of adhesive plaster, and were holding them up by the two ends.

Here I found Doctor Gunning, and to him I communicated the necessity of sending a party for the two men I had discovered with broken legs, and before I quitted the village of Columbeira, I had the satisfaction of seeing those poor fellows brought in, when I received their cordial thanks. Gunning, on seeing them, assured me those of the wounded who required amputations, and who had been out all night in the rain or dew without food, were far more likely to bear the amputations well, and with less after-risk, than those men who were operated on immediately.

I was soon informed of the address of Captain Elphingstone; and I found him in a tolerably comfortable house, up stairs, and lying in bed, his face bandaged; a slate was by his side, on which he communicated in writing. He thus acquainted me, that whilst engaged in looking at the enemy through his telescope a shot had struck him on the point of his chin, which, in fracturing his jaw-bone up to his ears, had knocked out three of his lower front teeth, which had gone down his throat; the ball then lodged under his tongue. Elphingstone proceeded to inform me that this wound did not cause him much pain; but he had, at the same moment, been shot in the thigh, which, although the ball had merely grazed the skin, was exceedingly painful to him.

Having conversed for an hour with Elphingstone, during which time I received the benefit of his advice and recommendation, I departed to return to the army I had left on the heights.

On my way I enlarged and rendered more perfect the plan I had made of the ground during the action on the preceding day, by extending it over the country at that time occupied by the enemy; and as this necessarily required I should traverse in every direction a great portion of the ground, in consequence of the woods and under-brush, I was again obliged to submit to the painful sight of so many human bodies dreadfully mutilated, many of whom had evidently been placed in positions intended to excite merriment; but which could produce no other sensation than a conviction that the persons who had so occupied themselves, must have been divested of every human or proper moral feeling, and raised in me sentiments of the utmost horror and disgust, which are quite indescribable.

One was seated and held a drawn sabre in his hand, the point over his shoulder like a sentinel; into his mouth the handle of a wooden spoon had been thrust, whilst the bowl of it was filled with filth.

A second had been raised against the rocky side of the road, in a position nearly upright, with a book in his hands, retained there with the aid of a cord; and in his mouth had been crammed the hand and part of an arm, which had evidently been cut off from a dead body lying by his side.

These, and numerous other acts of the like kind, proved the extreme depravity of the diabolical wretches, who could have found a pleasure in treating their fellow-beings in a manner so revolting to our feelings.

Amongst my pursuits of this day I completed a semi-circular panoramic view of the ground on which the battle had been fought, drawn from the spot on which four wind-mills stood, and close to the place where the guns, under Robe, had opened on the French Artillery and Swiss Regiments with Shrapnell shells; the first time of their being used in a field engagement.

CHAPTER XI.

Disposing of the dead bodies—Administering the sacrament to the dying—Peasants putting to death those who had received the sacrament—A devil, not a woman—I provide for the safe delivery of the wounded man at the depôt of wounded men—I return to the spot where I had left the army; the whole was gone—I follow, and purchase a horse—Arrive at Lourinha—No supper—I had assumed the command of the Engineers—I now sought for Sir Arthur Wellesley—I go on at the head of the march with Spencer—Sent forward to report on the merits of the position at Vimieiro—I narrowly escape being made prisoner.

ON returning up the hills by the high road, I observed in the woods, at a short distance to my right, several peasants about one spot, apparently very busy, and others moving to and fro from that place towards other parts of the forest; my curiosity was now excited, and I proceeded to the ground on which they seemed to be so earnestly engaged. On approaching them I discovered they were kindly performing the last offices to the dead ; a large hole, about twenty feet square and about eight feet deep, had been made, into which thirty to forty of the natives were carrying the dead bodies.

I felt much pleased and thankful to these people, and having given them a Spanish dollar to be expended in wine, I hastened away to recover the high-road. I had not proceeded many yards when I observed a Roman Catholic priest in his canonicals, followed by some ten to twenty devout persons, most charitably administering the sacrament to all the wounded indiscriminately, who, on being asked if they were Christians, gave any signs of assent. I rejoiced at witnessing an act so purely religious and completely disinterested, and gave the priest a small sum to be put into the poor-box of his parish, and which he received with marks of great respect, and in return bestowed on me his blessing with the sign of the cross.

The reverend father had just imparted this last consolation to a poor creature I had noticed before with several mortal wounds in his body, and who seemed now to be actually in the agonies of death; for, although speechless, he writhed and heaved dreadfully; his face and hands severely convulsed. I remained, during some seconds, looking on this unfortunate being after the priest had departed, and I know not why, until my mind was almost stupified; but the priest had not proceeded in search of other objects on which to confer his good deeds many yards, when I was roused by the approach of another small party of peasants, several of them carrying drawn swords, and evidently following the steps of the priest.

These people held no conversation with each other, nor did they express any sentiment, nor did they even utter a single word, but with a ferocious look, straightly walked up to the dying man before me, and without an instant's pause pierced him through the heart two or three times, and followed the priest, repeating this work of charity.

I shall not attempt to describe the feelings which at this sight agitated my whole frame; though I was glad that the poor suffering man had ceased to feel such agonies as I had witnessed, I could have shot the men who had so deliberately committed the deed; it was, no doubt, an act of mercy, but it was highly repugnant to my feelings.

The distressing sights I had beheld, particularly along the high road, were such, that I resolved on endeavouring to avoid a repetition of them by making a short cut through the woods, as I knew that the road bent away to the right; I, therefore, struck out in that direction, and at random scrambled over some very rough ground with my half-starved pony, for he had not had a feed, except of green food, since the previous day.

I had nearly gained the top, when the voice of an Englishman, calling loudly for help, caught my ear. I pushed forward, leaving my pony, for it would have been hopeless to expect that such an animal, or indeed, any other on such ground, could have carried me up in time to be of service, in a case of so pressing a nature as it evidently was, by the repeated cries for help, and then of murder; I stopped not to fasten my pony, I knew he would not run away, and in a few seconds, through the under-brush, I saw a woman, one of the British nation too, with a large stone in her hand levelling a finishing blow at a poor fellow of the 9th or 45th Regiment, I do not now recollect to which he belonged.

This wretch was at the man's back, as he sat on the ground, having had one of his legs broken on the preceding day by a musket shot, and was, therefore, quite helpless. My sudden appearance for a moment suspended the course of this infernal creature, and she remained with her hand raised, grasping a stone as big as both her fists, pausing, no doubt, to consider how far my presence ought to check her murderous views; and during this momentary hesitation, from the opposite side, out of the thicket, a man stepped forth, whom I immediately perceived was a private soldier in the 5th battalion of the 60th Regiment.

His occupation was not doubtful; plunder had induced him to straggle from his corps and remain in the rear, and I sincerely hope, his cupidity was confined to the property of the dead. This man was a German, and he also, as well as myself, had seen the diabolical intent of the woman before us. My hand was still strongly grasping the hilt of my sword, which I had half drawn, with a determination of stopping by force the further progress of this fiend; but the German lost no time in considering, he ran up, his rifle half up to his shoulder, and without any parley or ceremony, merely muttering as he sprang upon her, " You be no fouman, py Got! you be de tifle!" he put his rifle close to her ear, and before I had had time to form any clear conjecture as to his views, the upper half of her head vanished, and was dispersed into atoms amongst the bushes, and her body in falling almost extended to the wounded soldier.

Under any other circumstances, such a sight would have filled me with horror; I, nevertheless, here shouted loudly "*Bravo!*" with the most ample satisfaction; and whilst I was engaged in giving the unfortunate man a drink of wine out of my canteen, who informed me that the woman had already struck him one desperate blow on the shoulder with the stone, because he would not submit peacefully to be plundered of every stitch he had on, my German was engaged in very deliberately reloading his rifle, and then having carefully untied the woman's apron, which was richly filled with watches, rings, and valuables of all kinds, he darted from the spot, and disappeared amongst the bushes, casting at me a ferocious glance.

I felt no disposition to remonstrate with the rifleman, or to pick a quarrel with him in any shape, for his situation was too desperate; and although he might not be willing to proceed on the offensive towards me, or any other individual, had I alluded to his absence from his corps, which, under the then existing circumstances, was a crime for which his life had become forfeited; he might, and most probably would, have availed himself of the absence of sufficient means of conviction, to treat me in the same summary way he had pursued towards the woman, by which he could have augmented the weight and value of his rich booty, without any risk of detection.

My chief consideration now, was to provide for the safety of the wounded man, whose life had been so opportunely saved from the merciless fury of the wretched creature lying at his back.

It soon occurred to my mind that either my friend of the Rifles, or some other marauder, might, perhaps, take a fancy to my saddle, bridle, pistols, &c., if they should fall in with my pony; I, therefore, resolved on immediately securing my property : so, assuring the man I should not leave him unprotected, I ran to the spot where I had left my pony, and as I was leading him away back to the place I had just before quitted, I met the priest whom I had seen administering the sacrament, with so much benevolence, to several of the wounded of both sides of the question ; he also had been attracted towards the spot by the cry for help, and the discharge of the rifle, and had hastened his steps to afford his best assistance.

As soon as the priest observed amongst the group of peasants following him some particular individuals, he called them up to him, and after a short conference, he turned to me, and said, "These men are persons on whom I may depend; they are true Christians, and I have desired them to carry this poor soldier to the depôt." I felt no doubt in regard to their integrity, but I was anxious to give those men a decided interest in the safe arrival of the wounded man in the depôt. In order to secure this object, I wrote in pencil on a sheet of paper, torn out of my sketch-book, requesting the bearers might be paid or receive a gratuity of two dollars, on the safe delivery of the soldier entrusted to their humanity, and that I should pay the amount as soon as claimed. It was not many days after this that the dollars were claimed, under proper certificate; so I remained satisfied that the object I had had in view had been accomplished.

Mid-day was now fast approaching; I therefore made the best of my way up the hills, and by inclining to the left, I very soon regained the high road. Having passed the village of Azambujeira, I soon discovered that the army had advanced. I took the right-hand road without delay, as in that direction I heard the incessant screaming of the ox-wains, or cars drawn by oxen, attached to the commissariat, and which, when many of them are moving on together, make a noise so loud that it may be heard at the distance of several miles.

This distressing noise is caused by the extraordinary practice of never greasing the wheels; and it is said by the peasants, that the oxen are cheered by this music, and will travel many miles further in a day with than without it.

Having overtaken, and with great difficulty passed on to the front of this enormous train of musical vehicles, I observed a Portuguese farmer mounted on a very good sort of horse, the best I had seen not in the possession of some of the army; and I immediately resolved on purchasing him, if possible. I was, however, labouring under a serious difficulty,—namely, the total insufficiency of funds, having but seven Spanish dollars in my pocket, whilst the Paymaster was at the distance of several miles a-head with the army. I, nevertheless, bargained for the horse, and, at length, concluded the purchase for the sum of twenty moidores, about twenty-eight pounds sterling, which was probably double the local value; but my extreme need was such, that I would have given a much greater amount rather than miss the chance of being really mounted.

I used every effort to induce the farmer to go on with me to Lorinhā, where I had ascertained the army was to halt; but he was immoveable on that point, and not one step in that direction could I persuade him to take.

Having no alternative, I now resolved on waiting on the place where I had made the purchase; and seating myself on the step at a cottage-door, I there remained, in the hope that some one might come up with cash sufficient to relieve me from my difficulty.

After much delay and numerous applications, without success, to the officers of the commissariat guard as they came up in succession, I, at length, perceived my friend Hunter, the Paymaster-General. "That's the man," thought I. "If any one in the army can extricate me from my perplexity, Hunter is the man!" not for a moment reflecting that although he was the Paymaster-General, yet that was no reason for his carrying in his pocket more money than other people; and, as I might have expected, so it turned out— Hunter also had but a few Spanish dollars in his pocket.

Having explained my awkward predicament, Hunter consented to sit down by my side until his treasure arrived. I shall never forget how tediously the time passed; car after car during the space of four hours went past, and our patience had been ten times exhausted, still the treasure car did not arrive. The farmer, too, began to insist on cancelling the bargain for his horse, and made some determined attempts to carry him off, alleging that he lived at a great distance across the country, which, he said, was constantly infested by banditti.

About this time my servants came up, and I had the good fortune to persuade the farmer to allow the horse to go with them. I thus felt my prize secured; and shortly after, the money was lent me by Hunter, who, by that act, conferred on me a favour which I never shall forget.

By this protracted delay, I had again the inconvenience of being in the rear of a train of waggons or cars, drawn by oxen, and extending along some miles of road, and which, through being very narrow, rendered it highly irksome and inconvenient, particularly as night was fast approaching. We, nevertheless, by great perseverance, succeeded in once more arriving at the front of the whole of them.

Night had completely set in when we entered a narrow and deep road overflowed with water to the depth of six inches to one foot, and so we continued during two or three hours, and it was not until nearly eleven o'clock that I found the park of artillery.

I was as hungry as a hunter, having had nothing to eat that day since the cup of tea at two o'clock in the morning. On coming up, I observed a circle of officers sitting on the ground, and some plates and dishes before them, which gave an increased stimulus to my already exquisitely sharpened appetite; let any one, therefore, judge of the severity of my disappointment, when, on seeing me, I heard a general burst of laughter and exclamation, —

"You are just come in time to be too late to partake of the best curried ducks we have ever tasted."

And as a proof of that assertion, the dish was pushed over to me as I sat myself down, and wherein I observed that one pinion of a wing was left, with which I scraped the dish as clean as if I had been old Towser, a well-known dog, kept at one of the three half-penny dining places in St. Giles's, whose office was to lick the plates clean for the use of the next customer.

Not a morsel of anything else could I obtain, not even a biscuit could be found in any one's haversack. The grog also was all gone, so I was contented, *por força*, with a glass of water, and lay down, having learnt from my servant that my new horse was safe, had been well fed, and, moreover, had had a new set of shoes, a very important advantage when on a march.

My thoughts were wholly engrossed by the satisfaction I anticipated in being well mounted on the following day. No one can imagine how severely I felt the necessity to which I was driven, of riding on the back of a creature in no respect better than a donkey.

On the following morning, 19th of August, after making up, as well I could on tea and biscuit, for my previous day's fasting, the army advanced at about the usual hour.

Mounted on my new horse, which I found quite a prize, I sought Sir Arthur Wellesley, to whom I reported the state and nature of Captain Elphinstone's wound, and also that I had employed myself on the preceding day in extending and perfecting a plan of the ground upon which the action of the 17th had been fought. Sir Arthur expressed himself pleased at my having made the plan, and desired that I should supply him with a copy, to be ready in time to go to England with the despatches;

and my report with regard to Captain Elphinstone's wound was satisfactory, as he hoped it would not deprive the army of his services.

Towards mid-day, having, through some circumstance I do not now remember, become separated from the Commander-in-Chief, I hastened forward to the head of line of march in expectation of there finding Sir Arthur, but he had not been seen there; I, therefore, rode on with General Spencer and his staff, amongst whom were Captain Preston, the Aide-de-Camp, and Lieutenant-Colonel Bathurst of the Quarter-Master-General's Department, and many others, including Captain Hardinge (Lord Hardinge), also on the Quarter-Master-General's staff. We had not proceeded together very far, when Bathurst, with whom I had been acquainted at Winchester, in 1803 and 1804, when attending His Royal Highness the Duke of Cumberland, asked me if I had not made a plan of the ground where the action of the 17th had been fought; and on my answering in the affirmative, and showing it to him, he pressed me very earnestly to let him have a copy of it, to which I replied I should willingly do so after the departure of the despatches, but, as Commanding Officer of the Engineers, I could not give away that which belonged to the corps.

Soon after this, riding by the side of General Spencer, and in conversing on many of the interesting points connected with the action near Roliça, we arrived on the brow of a high hill, overlooking a country to the Southward, which although not flat was much lower than that on which we were then advancing. Upon opening this extensive prospect, Spencer ordered me to ride on into the lower country, and pointing to a village a mile and a half distant at least, said, "Look about that neighbourhood and ascertain what its merits may be for the army to halt upon, with a view also to cover the debarcation of fresh troops, and particularly, if capable of being defended. You know, in short, what is required for a military position."

On receiving this order, I hastened forward at a gallop down the road, and passing a very conspicuous and picturesque clump of eight or ten pine-trees, standing by the road side, I soon arrived at and passed through the village of Vimieiro. Here the inhabitants were all silent, no *vivas* proclaimed a welcome, they all wore an air of mistrust and extreme anxiety; I went on, and passing over a small stone bridge across a rivulet, ascended some high ground in my front, where, seeing a peasant at his cottage door, I begged a drink of water. I was served with great alacrity, at the same time his wife presented me with a couple of fine water-melons, in return for which I compelled the peasant to accept of a few *vintems*.

The weather was exceedingly hot, and nothing could have been more refreshing than a water-melon.

I soon reached a convent of great length, facing the sea, at the Northern end of which I dismounted, and peeping cautiously round the corner, I observed a helmeted head peeping, in imitation of myself, from behind the corner at the opposite extremity.

Up to this moment I had not reflected on my very advanced position, for I must then have been at least two miles from the spot where I had left General Spencer; and at which time he had cautioned me to be on the look out, as the enemy might not be far distant. Moreover, the peasant who had given me the water-melons, had also warned me that some of the French cavalry, dressed in green, could not be very far off, for he had seen several patroling about within the last half hour. I now, therefore, could explain the cause of my seeing the mysterious helmet; upon which, having already eaten one of the melons, I threw away the other, and mounted my horse with all convenient dispatch; and as quickly was off at a full gallop in the direction exactly opposite to the one in which I had seen the gentleman peeping round the corner.

I had, however, been seen, and was, therefore, as instantly pursued; but having the start of at least one hundred yards, and being mounted on a horse that did credit to my judgment; it is clear, the two dragoons at my heels could have but little chance of coming up with me before I should be supported. After a chase of five hundred yards, they fired their carbines at me, as a last hope, and gave up the pursuit.

CHAPTER XI.

My recommendation is adopted—I have a marquee—Reconnoitre the surrounding country — I refuse to give Bathurst a copy of my plan of the ground on which the battle of the 17th was fought—A copy was, nevertheless, published — Robe acquaints me we shall be attacked to-morrow—The action commences—I cut a way for a Brigade of Artillery to pass out of the Park—Great disturbance amongst the ladies—An interesting event—The 50th Regiment —A good laugh at "Who bobs there?" — I serve Brigadier-General Anstruther as A.D.C. — Lieutenant-Colonel Taylor—The Drum-Major—Cavalry turned by Eliott's guns.

I SOON rejoined General Spencer, and having reported that in my opinion the ground he had directed me to examine was favourable as a military position, possessing the essential points he had stipulated for, adopting the village of Vimieiro as the centre; that near it there was a convenient spot for the Artillery, and a sufficient supply of good water in the Maciera, which moreover, was not wanting along the remainder of the position; the General said, " I am satisfied we cannot do better, particularly as from what you have said, it would cover the debarcation of troops arriving on the coast to reinforce the army and furnish supplies." Bathurst, during this time, had been very attentive to my communications, and I thought, somewhat with an air of jealousy, at the immediate adoption of my recommendation. The General, however, ordered him to make his arrangements for taking up the ground, and to form the army in two lines; the first, so as to cover Vimieiro by its right, and extending Northward to near the spot we were then upon; and the left of the second, upon a chain of hills to cover the rear of the first line, along a shot distance, at about three hundred yards from it, and then to extend to a considerable distance towards Lisbon, curving away towards the sea coast.

As Commandant of the Engineers, I had now the advantage of a marquee (without tent), which was soon erected in the Artillery park, on the left of Lieutenant-Colonel Robe's. The park was formed, as I had recommended it should be, near the river Maciera, from which, with the surrounding country, there was every necessary and useful means of débouchéring, and it was a fine level meadow. The Maciera, after serpentining through this flat space, winds thence between high and abrupt hills, with a rapid stream to the sea, a mile or more distant, and is there somewhat checked by a bar of sand and gravel extending across its mouth.

As soon after our arrival as it could be prepared, we sat down to our usual dinner, composed of freshly killed beef, boiled, or rather stewed, with such vegetables as could be obtained; and copious slices of pumpkin were never wanting. Early rising, scanty breakfasts, and constant exposure to the open air invariably secured abundant praises of the produce of our camp kettle. The grapes being at this season ripe, we strolled away to eat our desert in the vineyards; and one of our morning reconnoissance was to ascertain where we could, after dinner, find a field of muscatels. I occupied the remainder of the day in making myself master of the details of the surrounding country as far as was prudent, and thus gained a good knowledge of the facilities or difficulties of communicating from the park in particular with every part of our position. By the time I had accomplished these objects, both myself and my horse were well disposed to rest; so that after our usual cup of tea, and then at eight a glass of rum and water, I retired to enjoy the comfort of having a piece of canvas betwixt the sky and myself; under which, I freely admitted as many of my own officers and of the Artillery as could find room. Amongst them I remember came Doctor Kenning, and Mr. Stace, the Commissary of the Artillery. I, this night, had a most refreshing sleep, being freed from the constant terror of being trampled to death by the horses that invariably, during the night, never failed to release themselves from their pickets.

On the following morning (20th August), soon after the early parade had been dismissed, Captain Maw, Assistant-Acting-Deputy-Quarter-Master-General, and whom I had known as a Sub in the 6th Regiment, came to me with a very sorrowful countenance, begging I would allow him to make a copy of my plan of the ground, on which the action of the 17th instant had been fought; and in order to strengthen his application, he added that he had been ordered by Lieutenant-Colonel Bathurst, Assistant-Deputy-Quarter-Master-General, to obtain it from me, if possible. He was probably not aware of my having on the day previous distinctly refused to give Bathurst a copy, until after the departure of the despatches, he having without disguise stated that he wanted it to send with those despatches; and he loudly complained at the same time of the gross neglect of the officers of his department, in having omitted to make a sketch of the ground during the action, as I had done. On my giving Maw a hint to the above effect, he perceived that he could no longer entertain any hope of succeeding in his mission, which caused him to express himself greatly disappointed, and he appeared exceedingly distressed; upon which, as a last effort, he exclaimed, "Do, my dear fellow, for God's sake! for old acquaintance's sake! pray let me have it, to save me from the certainty of being made a prisoner. You will hardly believe it possible that that Turk Bathurst (who is in a most violent rage with me for not having thought of making a sketch of the ground, when he himself had never dreamt of it, before he saw you had done it), has ordered me to go back and do it now, whilst every body knows that the whole of the ground is overrun by the enemy's cavalry from Peniché."

I was very sincerely affected at the risk to which he was ordered to expose himself, and assured him of my friendship; but I could not be induced to part with the sketch, which I repeated was the property of the corps. I therefore immediately delivered it to Sir Arthur Wellesley, to be sent home with the despatches, and His Excellency appeared to receive it with much satisfaction. This plan, or one exceedingly like it, and containing some errors which I discovered afterwards had crept into mine, was lithographed, containing the same errors, and issued, dated Horse Guards, Quarter-Master-General's Department; but my signature, which I had affixed to the original, was omitted in the lithograph. I then occupied myself principally in reconnoitring the surrounding country, which I repeated or continued after dinner, and did not return to my marquee in the Artillery park until nearly ten o'clock, when I was informed that Robe and myself had been sent for to attend at headquarters at about eight o'clock. Robe had been to head quarters and returned before I came in, when he immediately called me aside and said that I had been sent for to attend at head quarters with all the other commanding officers, and that my absence had not been commented on; but that Sir Arthur Wellesley had desired him to acquaint me that to-morrow we should be attacked, and therefore I must make any arrangements I might think necessary to meet that event; and he particularly enjoined that the strictest secresy must be observed.

The secret was properly kept from the army in general. Robe and myself made such preparations as regarded our respective departments, and at nearly eleven o'clock, just before I was about to lie down to rest, I stepped out to the front of my marquee, whence all appeared to be perfectly quiet, the sky beautifully clear, and not a breath of wind blowing; I could not help thinking, as I cast a look around our camp or bivouac, on the chances of the morrow : " Many of those," thought I, " who are now wrapped in tranquil sleep, and perhaps enjoying the most pleasing dreams of returning to the arms of those whom they best love, will never sleep or dream again, but in that sleep whence none awaken."

I turned away from these melancholy reflections, and soon stretched myself on the ground, without taking off hat, sword, sash, or spy-glass, a practice which I had uniformly observed from the first day of the march.

With some difficulty I fell asleep, but then rested well until the bugle called me to parade at a short time before break of day (21st of August, 1808).

At between seven and eight o'clock some distant firing of small arms announced that the advanced pickets were engaged, and that the information Sir Arthur Wellesley had received on the preceding day, and which he had communicated to us, was correct.

Every thing was now in movement, the drums were beating to arms, &c.; a brigade of guns being required to proceed out of the park to join the left wing, I found it necessary to fill up a hollow road close at hand, for which purpose I employed my own very small number of men, and collected a few more from the Irish Commissariat corps. This work took up nearly half-an-hour, during which time the enemy's Light Infantry had pressed forward with so much vigour, that although the work on which we were engaged was at least three hundred yards in the rear of the line, the musket shot occasionally dropped in amongst us; when one of them passing through the shovel of one of the Commissariat men, he threw it down, as if it had suddenly become red hot and had burnt his hands, and with extreme terror painted in his looks, after wildly staring at the shovel for a second or two, he screeched out, "Ah, murder!" and ran off as fast as legs could carry him.

At this moment I heard, in the direction of the valley leading to the sea, a strange uproar and confusion of female voices; and soon discovered running towards me, by the side of the Maciera rivulet, a great many women, perhaps thirty to forty in number, no doubt the wives of some of our soldiers. As they approached, it was perceptible that an event greatly irritating their temper had occurred; and all I could make out, for they all spoke at once, was, that they were heaping violent execrations, and most desperate menaces against a party not then mentioned or invisible. At length, when one of them came sufficiently near to me, I inquired into the cause of so much uproar and disturbance; "Fait, and I tink we have had enough to make us cry murder; warn't we all washing, down dare in de river, as safe, we taught, as if we had been on de banks of dear Channon, when we was all pounced upon by a party of French dragoons. The villains was not satisfied with taking the biggest liberties with us, but had the impudence afterwards to rob us of our shoes, which plaise your honour," she continued, " was a dirty, unmanly, mean, vile, cowardly, blackguard, ungentlemanly trick, to pass off on us poor harmless creatures, who had never once given dem an ugly word." On my making some remark on the first part of their grievance, she repeated, louder than before, " Ough de dirty villains! to take away our shoes was worse nor anything!"

By this time the way across the hollow road had been completed, and having seen the brigade pass safely over, although they sunk a little into the newly-filled earth; I mounted my horse, which had been waiting for me in the park, and rode off towards the two windmills, where I saw the reserve guns had taken up a position, commanded by Morrison under

Robe, and which induced me to believe that I should there find Sir Arthur Wellesley.

In order to reach that place, I necessarily passed through the village of Vimieiro; the shutters and doors of all the houses were closed, yet here and there, a face expressive of great anxiety was seen peeping through a shutter partly, and as if very cautiously, opened. At one of these, I saw a very interesting young woman with an infant in her arms, and on my stopping my horse and looking at her attentively, she beckoned me to her. On my approaching the window, she immediately begged I would advise her whether she should remain in the village or seek a place of safety at some distance, at least so I understood her from the signs and expressions of her features; as she pronounced the last words a cannon shot passed through the lower part of the house, upon which she uttered a piercing shriek, and ran from the window. Having waited a few moments without seeing her again, I rode off to the reserve guns, and never heard any further details of this event, for in the afternoon I found the house quite abandoned.

In vain I inquired after Sir Arthur Wellesley, as I was very desirous of joining him, but no one could give me any information as to where I should be likely to meet with him; I therefore remained with the reserve guns, thinking that the place to which he would most probably direct his attention.

I was much pleased and surprised at the readiness with which my horse's nerves had been reconciled to the violent explosions of Artillery, for after a few shots had been fired, he became perfectly steady; but as soon as the 50th Regiment, behind which I happened to be in conversation with their commandant, Colonel G. Walker, began a running fire, the poor animal was greatly agitated, and made various attempts to run off with me towards the rear.

The 50th were in line, on the right of the reserve guns, and just sufficiently retired from the crest of the hill to be out of sight of the enemy; and instead of advancing in line, or by divisions or companies, to fire on the enemy, each man advanced singly when he had loaded, so as to see into the valley, and fired, on having taken his aim; he then fell back into his place to reload. By this management the enemy concluded that the guns were supported by a small number of Light Infantry only, and were manœuvring at a long musket range, on some hills much inferior in height to those we occupied, and making their arrangements for the attack.

At this time some circumstance drew my attention towards the rear, and at a short distance to the right, where I found the 9th Regiment in columns of companies at quarter distances, with the left in front. The musket shots were whistling over our heads in great abundance, as I was walking my horse along the right of that regiment, when a shot having tickled the feather of one of the men, about the centre of a division, he stooped, or, as is usually called, bobbed. The officer on the right, who was standing a pace or two in advance, and whose vigilant eye was directed along the front of his division, was greatly offended at this involuntary movement, and called out with a stern voice, and great severity of aspect, "Who is that I see bobbing there? What are you bobbing about, sir? Let me see you bob again, sir, and I'll—." This severe rebuke was exceedingly proper, and would have had its desired effect, had not a cannon shot, or howitzer shell, I know not which, at this most critical moment, just as he had commenced his threat with "I'll—" whizzed over the officer's head. The noise made by such a missile, when passing within a yard or so of a person's head, is, to say the least of it, exceedingly disagreeable, and the stoutest nerves would not always save the individual from this highly reprehensible bobbing; so down went my officer a yard at least, but in an instant he had recovered his original erect position, having neither looked to the right nor to the left, his face the colour of his coat, his heart beating, ready to burst with rage at his own conduct, and wishing most sincerely that the shot or shell had taken off his head, and so have spared him the anguish he felt at being the first to deserve the mysterious punishment which he had, but three seconds before, half pronounced against the next bobber. By the rapidity with which he had recovered his position, he may at the instant have entertained a hope, his bob had not been noticed; if so, how keenly must he have felt his disappointment, for the whole of the front rank of the division in his rear had seen it, and also many of the men in his own company, which was instantly manifested by each of them muttering, "Who is that I see bobbing there? What are you bobbing about, sir?" and then adding, "Who bobs now?"

Having returned to the vicinity of the reserve guns and the 50th Regiment, and being without any fixed pursuit, Brigadier-General Anstruther, observing my want of occupation, and his Aide-de-camp's horse having been killed, called me to attend him to supply his place, adding at the same time, "I know that the officers of the corps of Royal Engineers have a particular objection to placing themselves under the orders of the Quarter-Master-General;" for the Brigadier-General was at that moment dressed in the uniform of the Quarter-Master-General; "but in this case," continued he, "I request your services merely as a Brigadier-General, without any reference to my position as Quarter-Master-General." I did not hesitate for a moment, and immediately followed him.

Nearly about this moment Lieutenant-Colonel Taylor, commanding the 20th Light Dragoons, came up to us on a fine prancing horse. Taylor was a particularly handsome fellow; and, as he approached, I perceived that he had been shot through the thigh. Since the commencement of the march we had been very much together, and had found him an agreeable companion; I now pressed him very earnestly to have his wound dressed forthwith. Taylor, however, treated the affair as of little moment, and, as he tied a handkerchief round his thigh, he replied by saying, "It is of no consequence, for I am just going to make a charge; if I survive I shall have plenty of leisure for attending to that trifle; if I fall, I shall have spared myself some unnecessary trouble and pain."

Taylor charged immediately, and was killed in a few minutes after this conversation, he refusing, although surrounded by bayonets, to surrender as a prisoner-of-war.

The first order I received in my new staff situation as Aide-de-camp, was to watch the movements of some of the enemy's cavalry on our right, and as they were at a considerable distance, I found it necessary to use my glass; but the wind being very strong, I dismounted, with a view to obtain a rest to steady my hand. I first tried to support my glass on my saddle, but my horse was too unsteady; I then went to a windmill close by, where a drum-major and all his little fry were gathered and crowded together behind the mill, in hope of protecting themselves from shots. I could not behold these poor little fellows, pale, and with looks manifesting extreme anxiety, without experiencing many painful feelings.

I found it, however, impossible to rest my glass against the mill without disturbing the drum-major, who could not be persuaded to move more than his head and body, but not his feet or legs, by which my object was defeated. Upon this, in a rather pettish manner, I said to him, "Keep your skulking place, you coward! I shall not disturb you;" and I retired a few steps, endeavouring, under the shelter of the mill from the wind, to hold up my glass.

I had not withdrawn from the spot then occupied by the drum-major more than half a minute, when I heard a sharp slap, followed by a deep groan. I turned round and observed the unfortunate drum-major with his hand on his breast, and nearly bent double, suffering severe pain. I thought he had been shot through the body, but on removing his hand, I found a musket-ball, which had struck his cross-belt, having made a deep dent in it, without passing through; the poor fellow was led away, and I think I was afterwards informed that he had died in a few days in consequence of this contusion.

At length, I got a sergeant's halberd to support and steady my hand; and I soon perceived the head of a column of cavalry, winding round the end of a hill, as if endeavouring to turn our right flank, and so cut in between the first and the second lines; the latter was on a range of high ground, commanded by General Hill. Just at this time a few nine-pounders, loaded with spherical cases, fired by Captain

Eliott from the right of the second line and about two thousand yards distant from the cavalry, were so perfectly directed, and the fuzees cut with so much accuracy, that the cavalry turned round and effected a hasty retreat.

CHAPTER XII.

Column of attack—Severe fire—Robe's noble feelings and devotion—The column advances—The column attempts to deploy into line—Anstruther's address to the 43rd and 50th Regiments—Walker's order and then charge—It was a grand sight—I am ordered to hasten forward and bring back those who had gone on the pursuit—I find it very difficult to halt these troops and make them fall back—I join General Fane—A Rifleman selecting his victim—Capture of a gun—Fane's delight—Two French officers wounded, and in a gravel-pit—General Pillet—General Brénier.

I now reported to Anstruther this event, whom I found near the 50th Regiment and reserve guns; and my attention was quickly drawn to the formation of a large column of attack at a short distance to the left of our direct front.

The column was in close order, and appeared to consist of about five thousand Grenadiers, and was advancing upon the reserve guns in double quick time, covered by a swarm of Voltigeurs, the latter running up in the most daring manner to within twenty yards of the guns.

During the whole progress of this column, the artillery kept up a most destructive fire, each of the guns being loaded with a round shot, and over that a canister; and I could most distinctly perceive at every discharge that a complete lane was cut through the column from front to rear by the round shot, whilst the canister was committing dreadful carnage on the foremost ranks.

At this period, Lieutenant-Colonel Robe, commanding the Artillery, and near whom I happened to be, turned to me and observed, "You're a lucky fellow to be mounted, for by God! if something be not very quickly done, the enemy will, in a few minutes, have our guns, and we shall all be bayonetted."

"Then," said I, "order up your horse, and be ready for the worst." "No no!" exclaimed the gallant Robe, with scorn, "I'll neither leave my guns nor my gunners,—I'll share the fate of my brave boys, be it what it may." The words here recorded are *verbatim* those used by Robe in expressing his entire devotion to the service.

The enemy's column was now advancing in a most gallant style, the drum by the side beating the short taps, marking the double-quick time of the *pas-de-charge*. I could distinctly hear the officers in the ranks exhorting their men to persevere in the attack, by the constant expressions of "*en-avant—en-avant—en-avant, mes-amis*," and I could also distinguish the animated looks and gestures of the mounted officers, who, with raised swords, waving forwards, strongly manifested their impatience at the slowness of their advance, and to which they also loudly added every expression of sentiments, which they thought best calculated to urge their men to be firm in their attack and irresistible in their charge.

In this way, the enemy having very quickly

approached the guns to within sixty or seventy yards, they halted, and endeavoured to deploy and form their line, under cover of the Voltiguers. I was then by the side of Anstruther, to whom I said, " Sir, something must be done, or the position will be carried." When the General replied, "You are right;" and, without a moment's delay, he called out to the 43rd and 50th Regiments, as he raised his hat as one about to cheer, " Remember, my lads, the glorious 21st of March in Egypt ; this day must be another glorious 21st." I have no doubt that this appeal had its effect.

Walker immediately advanced his gallant 50th to the crest of the hill, where he gave the words, " *Ready, present !* and let every man fire when he has taken his aim." This order was most strictly obeyed, and produced a commencement of destruction and carnage which the enemy had not anticipated. Then Walker called out, raising his drawn sword and waving it high over his head, " Three cheers and charge, my fine fellows !" and away went this gallant regiment, huzzaing all the time of their charge down the hill, before the French had recovered from their astonishment at discovering that the guns were not unprotected by infantry, as I afterwards was informed they had up to that instant fully believed.

This rush forward was awfully grand; the enemy remained firm and almost motionless, until our men were within ten to twenty yards from them; then discharged a confused and ill-directed fire from some of the front ranks, for the line had not yet been formed to its full extent, and the rear were already breaking up and partially running off. The whole now turned round and started off, every man throwing away his arms and accoutrements, as also his knapsack, cap, and, in short, everything that could have obstructed his utmost speed; and thus a gallant column, which but a very few minutes before this moment had numbered five thousand, at least, of the stoutest hearts in that army, was repulsed, scattered, and completely thrown out of action. The dispersion of this column presented a most interesting and curious sight; the whole of them being dressed in white linen great-coats, gave them, whilst in confusion and running for their lives, exactly the appearance of an immense flock of sheep scampering away from the much-dreaded shepherd's dog.

The charge of the 50th had been followed by the 43rd Regiment, and, I believe, another; and after pursuing the fugitives to the distance of three hundred to four hundred yards, we gave up the chase, our people perceiving that they were losing ground, and it was not to be expected, that fully loaded as they were, they could overtake the others when totally relieved from any weight but their clothes; and, moreover, it must be kept in view, that there is a very important difference in the interests of the two parties so circumstanced,—one runs to save his life, the other runs to kill his enemy; the want of speed in the first costs him his life, the want of speed in the second merely robs him of the killing of his enemy, already disabled, and no longer in a position to do him further mischief.

Some of the regiments on the right of the 50th, after the charge of the latter, or simultaneously with it, having also charged or advanced in the pursuit of the flying and broken remnants of the column, which, but five minutes before, had presented so imposing a front, having gone on to a very imprudent distance in advance of the line, Anstruther ordered me to go with all possible speed, halt them, and bring them back.

The order I had just received was very important, and required that its delivery should be rendered as certain as possible; and as I felt that it was a service of some danger, since the enemy's light troops were pressing forward on each side with a view to cut off the regiment to which I was to carry the order, I pointed this out to the General, and requested he would send off his orderly dragoon at the same time with a duplicate of the order, to secure the delivery of this important communication.

I started accordingly with as much haste as my horse could make down a steep hill, and over a very broken gravelly surface; and, as I had expected, the cross fire, which was immediately concentrated on the dragoon and myself, was such as left me but little hope that either of us could possibly reach our destination, for, with regret, I perceived the regiment I was endeavouring to overtake was pushing on after the flying enemy, without reflecting on the risk to which they were exposed by extending their distance from the main line.

This regiment had advanced half a mile or more, when I came up with them in a wood. On my way thither, soon after I had started, my pocket-book fell out from between my coat and waistcoat, where I had placed it, thinking that my sash would be sufficient to keep it in, although there was no pocket. As the book fell I discovered it, and called to the orderly dragoon to take it up, and I went on. This unfortunate fellow soon after came up to me in the wood, and delivering the book with his left hand, I observed that his right was up to his mouth, and he then drew out the stump of his forefinger, which had been, as he informed me, shot off at the moment he was picking up my book. The man was as pale as a sheet, and in the next moment fainted, and fell from his horse. I left him in the hands of the regimental surgeon, and never afterwards heard of him.

I found it no easy matter to enforce a halt. It is true, I had no charge of that nature; I might have rested satisfied with having delivered the order to the officer commanding, and ridden off; but seeing the importance of the case, and quickly discovering the difficulty the commanding officer had to contend with in enforcing the halt, I offered to assist him, which he most gladly accepted; and it was not before we had ridden up and down the line several times, delivering the order to every officer and non-commissioned officer separately, that the pursuit was abandoned.

The regiment was at that time much broken as to line, and almost intermixed with the enemy, partly occasioned by the quantity of under-brush, and partly by the eagerness of the men, which, under such circumstances, it is very difficult to restrain. I could very distinctly hear the shot striking the trees, and saw showers of the small branches and leaves cut away and dropping in every direction.

Having succeeded in carrying my orders into effect, and the regiment commencing its retreat towards the point whence it had started,

I made off to report to Anstruther; and on my way I found a regiment in line in the valley, which, I believe, was the 52nd, midway betwixt us and the position we had occupied from the commencement. Upon going up to the officer commanding, who was dismounted, I observed he had a white handkerchief wound round his hand; and on my expressing a hope that he was not severely hurt, he stated that he had received a shot through the palm of his hand, as he raised it over his head, huzzaing at the moment of charging the enemy.

This regiment had been sent forward to occupy the ground, and prevent the Light-Infantry from cutting off the retreat of the regiment which I had just before succeeded in halting.

On returning to the place where I had left Anstruther, I could see nothing of him, but I was informed that he had gone off towards the left. Accordingly I went away in that direction, and unwilling to waste much more time in vainly hunting about for him, and falling in with Fane's Light Infantry, who were actively engaged in driving back the enemy's Voltigeurs, I joined my old friends, and in a very few minutes I observed a Frenchman amongst the bushes, not more than sixty to eighty yards distant, shifting about from one concealing place to another, and at length I perceived him taking up a convenient position for giving me a proof of his abilities as a marksman. At the same moment I perceived just under my horse's nose a man of the 5th battalion of the 60th Regiment, belonging to Fane's brigade, and whose German countenance I recognized. Upon this, I called to him, "Do you not see that rascal taking his aim at me? Fire at him quickly, if you do not, he will hit me to a certainty."

A mounted officer amidst a parcel of riflemen stands but a bad chance of escaping, for he alone is visible, and seems to be put up as a target for the enemy to shoot at, whilst the privates or riflemen are all creeping about with so much industry in trying to conceal themselves, particularly the foreigners; and it has been observed that a German or a Prussian *jäger* will make himself quite comfortable behind a cabbage, a pumpkin, or even a large turnip, and there remain for hours, if he have the opportunity, dogging his prey, and that, too, without the least chance of being seen.

My friend of the 60th, however, had other views of greater interest to him than my life; for after repeatedly pressing and then ordering him to knock off the Voltigeur, who was taking so much pains to prevent me from becoming grey-headed in the service, he pettishly and half turning round, said, "Silence! ton't tisturp me; I want de officeer."

"Why do you want to kill the officer," cried I, "you rascal?" with as much vexation as he had manifested.

"Pecaus ter pe more plunder," muttered the wretch, keeping his eyes fixed on the object of his ambition.

It now immediately occurred to my mind, that, as we were rapidly driving back the enemy, this worthy had calculated on permitting the Voltigeur to pick me off, whilst he should return the compliment on the French officer; and thus secure the advantage of plundering me first, trusting to the almost certainty of getting up to the enemy before the French officer's carcase should be stripped by his friends, whose life he was unwilling to endanger.

All this was the work of a very few minutes, and my attention was attracted into a ravine or ground somewhat lower than the rest; wherein, by some circumstance with which I never became acquainted, one of the enemy's guns had been passed by the charging of our troops, and as by this time the conductors thought they might dash off and so escape from our hands, they started at a full gallop. I no sooner perceived this, than I set off in pursuit, and as my course lay close by General Fane and his Aide-de-camp, in passing I called to the General to follow and assist, which he forthwith obeyed, as if I had been his Commander; Captain Bringhurst, Brigade-Major McLean, and the General's orderly, with the General, quickly came up, and we instantly attacked the drivers as we rode by their sides. I swore at them in the French language, declaring if they did not pull up immediately, I should cut down the wheel horse postilion, raising my sabre over my left shoulder with that intention; and I have no doubt I should have carried my threat into execution, for the drivers, instead of slackening their pace at this, applied the whips and spurs with increased vigour, but just as I was nearing the wheel horse's postilion, and on his left-hand side, General Fane fired his pistol into the off-horse, which almost instantly brought him to the ground, and by that means the other horses were nearly all thrown down, and the gun itself narrowly escaped being overturned.

Fane was so delighted at this event, that he called for a piece of chalk ; but none could be found, which he much regretted, as he had been anxious to write the names of those individuals on the carriage who had absolutely captured the gun.

On the same spot was scattered a vast quantity of broken muskets, accoutrements, &c., and amongst them were also a great number of red and green feathers, mounted on whalebone, a yard long at least. The Genera picked up several of the green feathers, and having put one of them into his own hat, he handed one to me, saying, "There, my boy, wear that feather—you have rendered yourself worthy of being a Light Infantry man;" and gave me a most hearty shake by the hand. It will be recollected, that I had served with the Light Brigade under Fane's command, from the first day of our leaving the coast up to the 17th of August, when, by Elphingstone's wound, I had assumed the command of the Engineers.

At a short distance further down the hill, and in a small gravel pit, not more than eight or ten feet deep, I observed two French officers lying on the ground and unable to move; on seeing me they called out for help, and made signs for me to go to them. I was willing to afford them every assistance and protection in my power; so, without hesitation, I rode round the pit to the lower side, and inquired of them in what manner they were wounded; when I was informed, that one of them, in running from our bayonets, to save himself had leaped into the gravel pit, and had thus broken his thigh; and the other had been shot through the leg just as he was about to jump, and had, thereon, been precipitated into the pit. I assured them that I should exert my best efforts to afford them the earliest assistance and protection under existing circumstances, but, as they must be aware, some time must elapse before they could be carried away to the depôt for wounded, and so be placed out of the risk of being plundered, I begged of them that, if they had any thing of value about them they would entrust it to my care, and that I would most readily return it as soon as they should be rescued from the certainty of being robbed, to which they must continue to be exposed so long as they remained in the field; and that, probably, before the expiration of ten minutes they would be robbed of everything.

My proposition did not fail to excite some suspicions in the minds of these wounded and helpless men, which I admit it was well calculated to produce; but after casting a silent yet doubting look at me, they began to consult in the French language very freely, although they must have been aware that I perfectly understood every word they were pronouncing. Upon this, one of them observed to the other, "We must be robbed, that is clear enough, if we refuse this offer; it is better to take the word of an officer than to trust to the distant chance of escaping unobserved." The officer to whom this dialogue had been addressed, nodded assent, when both drew forth from under their waistcoats a broad and very heavy leathern belt, and having dismounted, I received them, saying to them, "Whenever you are so situated as to wish to repossess these treasures, for I presume, from the weight, these belts are well filled with gold, you may simply request that the Commanding Officer of the Engineers be sent to you, and I shall have much pleasure in attending to your wishes." The announcement of my station in the army relieved them from any doubts as to the security of their property, and drew from them repeated expressions of gratitude. Having buckled the two belts round my waist, I mounted and trotted off.

Anxious to rescue these two officers from their painful situation, and to prevent them, if possible, from being plundered of any property remaining on their persons, I hastened up the hill to near the windmills, and there mentioned their fate to such surgeons as I met, and directed a Serjeant to proceed to the spot which I pointed out, and with a party to bring them up to the position occupied by the reserve Artillery, about which the wounded were ordered to be collected until otherwise disposed of.

I there saw General Pillet, the French Adjutant General, he was lying on the ground, wounded in the right hip, and Doctor Fitzpatrick of the Ordnance Medical Department, was engaged in endeavouring to extract the ball, but I believe he could not find it.

Soon after this, and on the same ground, I saw a French officer who was wounded in the ancle or foot, which was tied up in a handkerchief, he was without a hat, on a horse, and a man held the bridle leading him off; I was informed he was immediately shipped off to England. His hair was nearly red, and I understood that this officer was General Brénier.

CHAPTER XIII.

The French show a line—The space betwixt us—A soldier of the 50th gives me a silver dish—The dirty half hundred becomes the gallant 50th—The field of battle—Fear of poison—Morrison's hat shot through, the same as my own—Shot at by a wounded prisoner —I return the compliment—I find Sir Arthur—Torrens' account of Mulcaster's conduct—Colonel Burn— Lieutenant Price—Sir Harry Burrard—I am introduced by Sir Arthur—Conversation with Sir Harry— Sir Arthur presses Sir Harry to go on—Sir Arthur's conduct thereon.—Sir Harry is hungry and wants his dinner—Thomas Robinson's determination to save the gravy—Some plunder of French baggage waggons.

THE firing had now almost totally ceased, and the enemy was actively engaged in collecting his scattered troops, and in reforming them into line in order to make as formidable an appearance as the general disaster which he had experienced at all points, could enable him to accomplish. In this way, Junot, the Duke of Abrantes, contrived to show us a line drawn up on a range of hills parallel to our position, and at the distance of a mile or more, with a view, no doubt, of being regulated in his further movements by those we might adopt.

The ground between us was variously scattered over with killed, wounded, arms, drums, caps, knapsacks, canteens, dead horses, and ammunition waggons, and some cannon; but the track, which the before-mentioned column of attack had followed, was conspicuously marked to a great distance, by the number of killed and wounded, who had fallen by our Artillery in its progress towards us, and which regularly increased in numbers as the column had approached; at the extreme point of its advance, where an attempt had been made to deploy and form the line, the dead and dying were, in some places absolutely lying in heaps, three or four men in height. The wounds of nearly the whole of these being inflicted by cannon-shot, were, as it may be supposed, truly horrible, and of every possible variety.

Observing a baggage waggon, two or three hundred yards in advance, which was surrounded by a number of soldiers and women, I rode on towards it, not with any intention of gaining any portion of the plunder, but guided by mere curiosity. The contents on my arrival had already been tolerably well dispersed, amongst the fifty or one hundred individuals, scrambling, and in some cases fighting, for some of the most valuable articles. A man of the 50th Regiment, who appeared to have been exceedingly successful, for he was fully loaded, on recognising me, came up, and thrusting into my hand a small but handsome silver dish, addressed me in the following manner :—
" There, companion in the most glorious charge ever made in this world, take this, you have not had a plate at your dinner since we landed, I know, that will do for one; and remember that it was the *dirty half-hundred* that won the victory this day." I must here explain that the uniform of the 50th Regiment was red,

faced with black and silver lace, which sombre colours, or bad assortment, gave the regiment at all times an uncleanly appearance, whence it had been denominated the Dirty 50th, or Dirty Half-hundred; but ever after this glorious charge led on by Colonel Walker, (since General Sir George Walker, G.C.B., and lately Commander-in-chief at Bombay,) the Dirty Half-hundred has been dismissed, and in its place stands the gallant 50th.

Not far from the waggon, I found a very handsome oiled silk cloak lined with blue silk, lying tied up half concealed in a furze bush; I soon after this gave it away, but do not remember my motive for parting with an article which I so much required, for I had no great coat.

I was here in the midst of the wreck of war, and in the place where the action had been the severest, whence, casting a look around, my attention was quickly attracted by observing a number of soldiers, women, and peasants, eagerly pursuing, and using every exertion to capture, several horses with their saddles and bridles still on, and a few that had belonged to the

French Artillery, with portions of harness hanging about them. Another party I observed were engaged in knocking the shoes off the dead horses, an article at this time in great demand throughout the army.

Whilst all these various and highly interesting events were occurring, in every direction over the field of battle, that had remained in our hands, I noticed our soldiers zealously emptying every canteen they could find that had belonged to the enemy. On enquiring the motive for which this was done, I was informed, that it was certain that the French had poisoned the contents of their canteens, in order to destroy the British soldiers who might capture them. This was a story no doubt invented with a view to prevent our men from drinking to excess, for each of these canteens contained from two to three pints of brandy, and may account for the vast number of the French soldiers who were made prisoners on that day, being evidently more than half drunk.

Having returned towards the top of the hill, where Robe's reserve guns had experienced such a narrow escape, I there observed my friend Captain Morrison of the Royal Artillery, and I believe that I was the first who noticed to him that his cocked hat had been shot through, just over the back of his head; and which had torn it much more than was sufficient for the passage of a grape shot, which I suppose it was that had so nearly killed him; and at the same moment he was the first to acquaint me with my having received a shot, probably from a rifle, through my hat, and exactly in the same part of it.

I now went on, and came up with Colonel Walker, whom I joined, he was mounted on his white horse; and we were conversing on the brilliant results of his charge, when I heard a musket discharged from our rear, and at the same moment a shot whizzed close to our heads. I quickly turned round, and the smoke guided me to a wounded man, a prisoner, sitting up, and slyly putting down a musket.

It is almost needless for me to state that I felt greatly exasperated at the murderous intent of such a villain, and but little compassion at his wounded condition; so having galloped close up to him, as I drew forth one of my pistols, I pulled up my horse in order to take a more certain aim, upon which, as soon as he discovered my preparations to punish his cowardly attempt he contrived to get on his knees, and roared out for mercy in a very frightful manner, his eyes I well recollect, almost started out of their sockets. I nevertheless fired my pistol at his breast when not more than three yards distant from him.

To my extreme surprise the man did not fall, but retained his posture, which perplexed me beyond all power of description, and whilst I remained staring with astonishment at the man, his eyes were idiotically fixed on me. At length being perfectly convinced that I had not hurt him, I turned away rather pleased, I think, but certainly not angry with myself at my clumsiness in missing him, saying to him in French, as I moved off, " Well! you have had a shot at me, and I have had one at you, we are therefore quits."

The whole of this event had been witnessed by a vast number of the enemy's wounded, who to a man insisted on a summary execution of the dastardly prisoner, heaping on him the bitterest reproaches and execrations, no doubt fearing that such conduct might be the cause of visiting them with an unusual degree of severity.

Up to this time I had not seen, nor could I obtain any information of Sir Arthur Wellesley. I was now accidentally informed that he had been during the whole of the morning, at or about the extreme left with Major-General Ferguson, I immediately directed my steps to join His Excellency; but I had not proceeded far, perhaps not more than one hundred yards beyond the very remarkable clump of eight to ten pine trees, already mentioned, close by the side of the road leading to Lorinhā, when I met Sir Arthur and staff, and amongst them Lieutenant Mulcaster, my adjutant.

Without the loss of a moment I stated to Sir Arthur how I had been employed, and accounted for my absence from His Excellency, upon which he expressed himself perfectly satisfied.

I now resolved on not losing sight of the

Commander-in-Chief for a moment, and therefore took up my place in his suit, following Sir Arthur back to the ground I had been on during the whole of the action.

In riding on, Lieutenant-Colonel Torrens, who was the Military Secretary, gave me the following account of Mulcaster's very gallant conduct:—

It happened that at one period of the action, Sir Arthur was watching with particular attention and interest some of the movements of the enemy, and was at that moment on the brow of an elevated position, and during this time the enemy's Light Infantry, or Voltiguers, were creeping up the hill amongst the bushes, and firing very deliberately at Sir Arthur and his staff.

Mulcaster had with anxiety been watching these riflemen, and fearing that, unless they were quickly disturbed, they would very soon succeed in hitting the Commander-in-Chief, he went up to Sir Arthur, and in the most respectful manner, pointed out his danger, but of which the only notice taken of his good intention was, "Very well, sir; I see them."

Sir Arthur, however, was too much otherwise engaged to remember Mulcaster's warning for a moment; and the enemy acquiring boldness at the indifference manifested towards them, continued to advance gradually; when, after several shot fired by these fellows, which had happily passed amongst the group without effect, Mulcaster repeated his communication, which, however well intended, rather annoyed Sir Arthur, by disturbing him in his observation, upon which his Excellency said, "Very well, sir; go then with such of the Dragoons as you can gather, and drive them back."

Though there was no Cavalry at hand, but the small number of orderly Dragoons (of the 20th Regiment), close in the rear, and belonging to the General's staff, yet, upon receiving the order, he called them up, and drawing his sword, ordered them to follow him, when, in a few minutes, having charged into them, he sabred some, and put the remainder to flight. On riding back, he reported to Sir Arthur that he had carried his commands into effect, which called forth a distinct approbation from the Commander-in-Chief.

Of the other little adventures which may have occurred in different parts of the line I have not had many opportunities of learning the details, or, perhaps, time has swept them from my memory. I shall, therefore, merely record that an officer of the 40th Regiment related to me that whilst with his Regiment in Major-General Ferguson's Brigade, stationed on the extreme left, and consisting of the 36th Regiment, commanded by Colonel Burn, the 40th by Colonel Kemmis, and the 71st under Colonel Denis Pack, the whole of the Brigade was ordered to sit down on the ground, somewhat retired from the crest of the hill, on which they were posted. By this measure the men were less exposed to shot; and very strict orders had been given, prohibiting the return of the enemy's fire under any pretence whatever, without express orders to do so. During this sort of pause, a musket belonging to one of the 36th was fired, probably by accident; upon which Colonel Burn, a man of quick temper, rode up to the spot, and being unable to detect the individual whose musket had been discharged, he exclaimed, " I only wish I could discover the rascal who has just fired off his musket against the most positive orders to the contrary, and I would give him a good caning, he may depend on it I would." The Colonel, all the time he was then addressing his men, flourishing the weapon at that portion of the line where he had observed the smoke of the discharged musket streaming off with the wind.

A few months after this I met Lieutenant Price, of the 52nd, at Santarem, who was then on the staff of Brigadier-General Richard Stewart, when he informed me that he had served with his regiment at the battle of Vimieiro; and that upon the occasion of the charge of the 50th, already noticed, he had encountered a private soldier of the enemy in single combat. Price for some time succeeded in maintaining his ground with his sabre against the persevering efforts of the Frenchman with his fixed bayonet, when, at length, in stepping backwards to avoid a rush which the man made at him, he fell on his back. The chance of escape for poor Price was now ten to one against him; yet the Frenchman missed his opportunity by being too hasty, for, in stabbing at his breast, Price received the bayonet through his right arm, just above the wrist, and it then passed through the upper part of the same arm; and such was the force with which the soldier had plunged the blow, that a considerable portion of the weapon entered the ground, and so literally pinned the English officer to the spot. In this posture the combatants remained during a few seconds, their eyes fixed on each other, and uttering execrations in their respective languages. The Frenchman was, no doubt, fearful of drawing out his bayonet, with a view of inflicting a more deadly wound, lest he should receive a cut on the head from Price's sabre, which he still firmly grasped; he, therefore, made every effort to injure his antagonist by kicks and stamps; and, whilst in this most critical state of affairs, Price was very opportunely rescued by one of his own men, who, having observed his peril, ran up to his aid, and in an instant shot the Frenchman through the head.

On arriving on the spot where Robe's reserve guns had been stationed, near the two windmills, and at a short distance from the village of Vimieiro, we came up to Lieutenant-General Sir Harry Burrard, whom I had neither seen nor ever heard of before that moment.

I was afterwards informed that Sir Harry had that morning landed from the ship which had brought him from England, and just as the firing was commencing; but that Sir Harry had most properly declined taking upon himself the command of the army, although senior to Sir Arthur, stating, that as Sir Arthur had made himself acquainted with the ground, had formed his line, and, in short, had actually commenced the action, he should not in any way interfere, but would accompany Sir Arthur, and would give him his advice, should he at any time request it. All this was exactly as it should be.

On our coming up to Sir Harry Burrard, I was introduced; upon which he said to me, "This is a glorious victory; we must have a plan of the ground, and of the movements of the troops, to be sent off with the despatches."

I promised the plan (for I knew it was making by the several officers under my command); and then added, in reply to the General's observation as to our having gained a glorious victory, that "we are in a fair way to gain a brilliant victory; the battle is very well commenced."

At this moment, Sir Arthur, who had been at too great a distance to hear my observation, came up, and pressed Sir Harry to order General Hill to move on towards Lisbon, adding, that his division was quite fresh, since the men had dined whilst the first line had been fighting; that they had not marched one step more than to take up the position they then occupied, and had not fired a single shot during that day. Sir Arthur made some further observations about the advantages we possessed, arising from local circumstances, and of momentary value only; but Sir Harry resisted every argument for advancing, by making some allusion to a conversation they had had on the preceding evening on board of the Brazen; after which, Sir Harry suddenly turned to me, repeating the necessity of my getting a plan for him of the operations immediately; then asking me what was the hour, and, without waiting my reply, inquired of Sir Arthur at what time his dinner would be ready, assuring us, as he tapped his full-sized waist two or three times with his open hand in a most inquisitive manner, that the sea air had very much sharpened his appetite.

On perceiving that Sir Harry Burrard had determined on not following up our advantages, Sir Arthur Wellesley reined in his horse four or five yards, dropped the bridle on his horse's neck, pulled down his cocked hat to the bridge of his nose, and having folded his arms, he drooped his head, and remained during some minutes in that position, evidently regretting that he could not follow his own opinion.

There can be no doubt that, had we pursued the advantages we had so far obtained, the enemy must before night have surrendered at discretion; yet all the time whilst Sir Arthur remained in that pensive position, Sir Harry went on talking half to me, and half to himself, when he several times repeated, "Well, I think we have done enough for one day;" to which I once or twice replied, "The victory is well commenced."

During the morning we had experienced several sharp showers from the South-West, and now the rain began to come down rather more briskly than before, when the two Lieutenant-Generals retired to Sir Arthur's quarters, and I trotted off to the artillery park, where I found that our dinner was on the point of being taken from the fire.

We all now met each other, as we dropped in at various periods, with a hearty shake of the hand, expressing very sincerely the pleasure in which we all participated at meeting again safe and sound after a very severe day's fighting, and that, too, without having to lament the loss of any officer of the Artillery, or of the Engineers. Lieutenant Wells was on that day made a prisoner; but we were already aware of his personal safety, though how we came by that information I do not now recollect.

Our excellent and usual stewed beef and vegetables very soon made its appearance.

Thomas Robinson, a Scotchman, and private in the Royal Artillery, and who was Robe's servant, was the *chéf-de-cuisine*, and we found the stew so excellent, that we almost devoured it, our appetite being remarkably keen. Praises were now heaped on Thomas without reserve, for he had never operated better, was the unanimous feeling, and so it was unanimously expressed.

Thomas was one of those stiff, hard-faced soldiers, with an air so stern as almost amounted to moroseness or sulkiness; was a man of few words, and such as he used were so blunt that any stranger would have thought him rude; but such was not the case—it was the result of uncultivated manners. He was honest and faithful to the letter, and brave beyond all doubt. Whatever duty he was ordered to perform, it was punctually executed. On hearing the expressions of approbation so profusely bestowed on him, Thomas manifested no visible sensation of pleasure, but, with a manner more expressive of anger or reproach than of satisfaction, he said:

" Weel, weel, you may think yur sells vary

lucky in having any gravy at all to the meat, for the shots was flying aboot so theck, that I axpacted every meenit one wud a gone thorough the kattle, so I beelt up a rampart, do ye see?" pointing to the semicircular bank of sods, about three feet high, round the fire; "and good it was vary weel that I thought o' that, for in lass than twa meenits so many shots cam'd reght into the building, that some of them wad a let oot a' the gravy, had it na been for the sods, do ye see?"

Upon hearing this declaration we all burst out roaring with laughter at the simplicity of the tale; yet we could not resist admiring the devotedness of this faithful servant, who had, regardless of his own safety, built up a bank of sods just of the dimensions sufficient to protect the kitchen, lest an unlucky shot might miss him, but tap the kettle.

During the time we were most agreeably engaged in satisfying the cravings of a ravenous appetite, reports were at very short intervals made to Robe of cannon, ammunition waggons, and artillery horses, that were bringing into he park of artillery, and which had been captured from the enemy; so that, I think, out of about twenty-two pieces of cannon which the enemy had brought into action that morning, seventeen or eighteen of them were before dark secured and brought in: these were as quickly entered upon the returns preparing, with the utmost exertion, to go off that evening with the despatches.

Amongst the various waggons brought in, one of them contained some baggage which had belonged to a French officer of Artillery, and which we immediately amused ourselves in plundering.

All I obtained was a sportsman's powder-flask made of horn, and which is still in my possession.

CHAPTER XIV.

I refuse a good offer—I write my despatch with an umbrella held over my paper—I deliver my plan of the battle to Sir Harry—Sir Harry made no mention of the Engineers in his despatch, nor did he of the Artillery, which Robe having discovered it in time, had corrected—The ball falls out of my pistol—More troops arrive—Robe's joy at the arrival of his son, but he was killed at Waterloo—A baggage-waggon plundered — An ammunition-car damaged — Sir H. Dalrymple arrives from Gibraltar, and I go to meet him—The drums beat to arms—The French General Kellerman arrives in the army with a flag of truce—March and bivouac on some wooded hills.

OUR spirits were greatly elevated, as it may be fairly expected, at the successful results of this day, and the quantity of cannon, ammunition, arms, accoutrements, horses, &c., captured, raised our expectations to a high degree, and we calculated on a handsome division of prize-money.

I began to feel the importance of being the commanding officer, since, instead of sharing merely according to my rank of Captain, I should be allowed to participate with the field-officers. Under this view of my prospects I refused an offer made me of fifty pounds, then of one hundred, and ultimately of one hundred guineas, for my share of the prize-money; and those who were present assured me that, in their judgment, I was quite right, for my portion could not be less than five hundred pounds. Such was the high value we expected would be the result of our victory.

I have since had reason to regret my not having caught at the offer; for, although a million sterling was afterwards voted by Parliament to be distributed to the troops that had served in the Peninsula, through some most unaccountable motive, and which I have never had explained, the services performed by the troops employed during the first campaign, although everywhere victorious, were not thought deserving of any recompense; we were, therefore, excluded, and so I received nothing.

I thought this particularly hard, after having participated so exclusively in capturing a field-piece, horses, and ammunition-car, all complete.

The remainder of the day I occupied in putting together the reports of the several officers of Engineers, with their sketches of the ground upon which they had been respectively engaged, and in writing my official despatch to the Inspector-General of Fortifications, letters to my family, &c.; the whole of which I was under the necessity of managing under the shelter of an old umbrella, which I had fortunately picked up in the field of battle, and which was held over my head to keep the paper from being wetted by the rain, which fell steadily during the whole of the time : my marquee had been struck at the commencement of the engagement, and having been carried off to the rear, was still away.

As soon as I had accomplished these important matters, I waited on Sir Harry Burrard, and having delivered to him the plan of the battle, he expressed himself very much satisfied with the expedition with which the same had been completed, and assured me he should make particular mention of me in his despatches; adding, "You may depend on my taking good care of your interests;" then, after a few more questions regarding the plan which I had been explaining, "I shall make such mention of your zeal and activity, as cannot fail to be duly noticed and appreciated in the proper quarter."

I now bounded, as I went down the narrow stairs. "Stand out of the way, every body; I am a Major, as sure as a gun, from this date," thought I, all the way I went in returning to the park.

Sir Harry did not mention my name, nor even did he take any notice of the corps of Royal Engineers in the despatches. Sir Harry Burrard had in like manner totally omitted to mention a single word about the Royal Artillery; but Robe, having had the good fortune to hear of it in time, waited on His Excellency immediately, when he demanded and obtained satisfaction, by a most honourable mention of the services which that corps had rendered, and had so justly deserved.

My marquee now made its appearance, just as dusk was commencing, and that I began to anticipate the probability of passing a dreary night in the open air, and getting a thorough wetting; and whilst it was erecting, I received a summons to attend at the church, where two wounded French officers were anxiously inquiring for the Commanding Officer of Engineers. I was in no degree perplexed as to whom the wounded officers could be; and I was much pleased at the receipt of this invitation, for I began to feel the inconvenience of carrying about my waist the two belts so heavily charged, together with my silver dish under my arm; and moreover, I looked forward with considerable anxiety to my being compelled to pass the night in the open air completely unprotected from the cupidity of several hundreds of men, whom I had observed had cast longing eyes at the quantity of wealth I carried about so visibly and invitingly displayed.

I therefore hastened to the church, and there

had the pleasure of restoring the heavy belts to the owners, who beheld my approach with unfeigned satisfaction.

After numerous expressions of their thankfulness, they acquainted me with their names and places of residence in France, and I believe that I made a note of them at the time; but I have lost any record which I may have made upon the subject, so I have never availed myself of their polite invitations to their homes, where I have no doubt I should have experienced a hearty welcome.

On my return to the park I not only found the marquee erected, but I was glad to notice that one of my servants, who had been missing with my baggage mule, which I had purchased on the preceding evening, had now made his appearance, but without the mule. The account he gave of himself was, that as soon as the firing had commenced, the mule started off, and he had gone in pursuit of it. The animal, he said, had led him a pretty chase all over the country, to the extent of several miles, when he was compelled, through fatigue and want of nourishment, to give up the search.

This story appeared to be a very lame one, and it was generally suspected that he had sold the mule, and that he had occupied himself in plundering the killed and wounded; for I afterwards was informed that he had been seen to have in his possession a large sum of money. On applying to the Board of Ordnance for the loss of this mule, I was informed, that unless I could declare that it had been killed or had fallen into the hands of the enemy, I could not be compensated.

Having procured a sufficient quantity of dried Indian corn leaves, to keep me from lying on the wet ground, I was making my arrangements for the night, before it should be quite dark, when my servant, who, in fact, was my groom, came in with my saddle and bridle, as I always used the former as a pillow; and he acquainted me, to my infinite sorrow, that my horse had received a shot in the inside of his thigh; and that the veterinary surgeon could not find the ball, which had evidently lodged at a considerable depth amongst the muscles.

My man soon afterwards, in removing my holsters, heard something rolling about, and on examination discovered that the ball of the pistol I had fired at the wounded prisoner, had previously fallen out into the holster, which at once unravelled the mystery of my having missed the man.

The constant tapping of the muzzle of the pistol on the bottom of the holster pipe, had no doubt occasioned the ball to fall out.

Fearful that on some future occasion, my life might be placed in jeopardy through a repetition of such an accident, I ordered two round pieces of wood to be procured and cut exactly of the length of the barrels left unoccupied by the charges, and sufficiently small not to fix or fasten in the barrels, but to remain in the holsters when the pistols were drawn out; thus the charges, by resting on these sticks, must ever remain in their places.

Having taken our tea as usual, an hour afterwards we drank a glass of rum and water to the health of our friends in England, and every one proceeded to take up his position for the night. Mr. Stace, of the Commissariat, and Doctor Kenning, both of the Ordnance department, had landed that day

MY MILITARY LIFE. 257

from England, and were glad to accept my invitation to take shelter under my marquee; which was constantly open, in like manner, for the comfort of as many as could therein find a place for their length and breadth.

During the battle, and, indeed, all the remainder of the day, troops were landed as fast as they arrived on the coast; and I had to commiserate with an officer of the 62nd Regiment, whom, at about nine o'clock in the morning, I had recognized as an acquaintance, on his joining from the sea-shore with his regiment, but who before two o'clock of the same day, and nearly on the same spot, I met on a litter, shot through the leg; he was then on his way back to his transport.

Amongst the arrivals on that day from home, was Lieutenant Robe, of the Artillery, who joined his father about the commencement of the action; and I remember the Lieutenant-Colonel saying to me, with tears of joy in his eyes, soon after the fighting had terminated, that his utmost desire had been gratified by the arrival of his eldest son on that morning, who had remained by his side throughout the engagement. "Oh, how happy am I that William, my dear boy, was here this day to share with me in the dangers and honours of this glorious battle." Robe repeated this to me over and over again, as I believe he expressed himself in the same way to many others; his heart was too full to be able to conceal his joy, which was completely overflowing.

Lieutenant Robe, seven years after this, was killed at the battle of Waterloo.

I had nearly omitted to mention an event which caused us much merriment during the evening of this day. On plundering the baggage of the French Artillery officer above-mentioned, Major Viney, of the Artillery, had seized on the Sunday coat, which, on leaving Lisbon, had been most carefully packed up, and which was decorated with a pair of epaulets, nearly new. This coat, Viney instantly put on, and it fitted him to a T. The novelty of seeing a French uniform amongst us, as he strutted about the park, was very amusing, but we considered it exceedingly inelegant.

Our sneers and objections to the style of uniform were particularly directed against the ill-judged position of the epaulets, which, instead of being as we then wore them, placed perfectly on the top of the shoulders, or, perhaps, rather in a slight degree more towards the back than the front, giving the man a very erect appearance, and a great expansion of chest, were placed very forward, as at present worn by the British army; and which is the cause of both officers and privates appearing to be round-shouldered, narrow-chested, and stooping or bending forwards.

From the moment when the sun had withdrawn its light, the Portuguese division serving with our army, and which, I believe, amounted to about five or six thousand men, had began to make bonfires; and were firing off their carbines and muskets at every instant, shouting, singing, and rioting in the most noisy manner, in manifestation of their joy at the severe overthrow which the French had on that day experienced from our troops.

This very unmilitary and unsoldier-like conduct, particularly when in camp before an enemy, was kept up until the bugle called us to the usual morning parade, notwithstanding every effort to procure its suppression.

At the usual time after daylight, the troops were dismissed, and there were no symptoms of advancing on that day.

After taking some breakfast, I went to inspect an ammunition car, which had been blown up during the action; and so little was it injured, that by this time it was quite ready to take its place in the line of march, if required. But what I considered very extraordinary, was, that neither the horses to which it was attached, nor the driver, at that time mounted on one of them, were in the slightest degree injured.

At about ten o'clock I paid my respects to the Commander-in-Chief; and whilst there, a communication was received, announcing that Lieutenant-General Sir Hew Dalrymple had arrived on the coast to assume the chief command, and was about to disembark.

Sir Arthur Wellesley immediately turned to me, and said, " Oh, you are acquainted with

Sir Hew—you were at Gibraltar under his command; you must go to the landing-place at the mouth of the river, and receive him and conduct him here."

In compliance with this order, I proceeded, and on my way was overtaken by Captain Cook, of the Adjutant-General's department, who was leading his handsome sorrel-coloured horse, and we went on together; he also having been dispatched to meet Sir Hew Dalrymple.

On our arrival at the beach, Sir Hew Dalrymple was just landing; and having announced the object of my mission, I showed his Excellency the way by leading my horse before him.

Sir Hew's staff consisted of Captains Dalrymple, his son and Military Secretary, Walsh, Blair, and Gibbons, of the Line, and Fanshaw, of the Royal Engineers, Aides-de-camp; and I believe there were one or two more. We very soon arrived at a small house, the quarters of Sir Harry Burrard; and here Sir Hew expressed some perplexity at being without his horses; when I suggested that the easiest way to get rid of that difficulty for the moment, would be to dismount a few of the Cavalry about Sir Harry's quarters, and that their horses would supply the deficiency.

My recommendation having been adopted, we all went on to join the army, which had not moved from the position occupied on the preceding day; and as we arrived in sight of the village of Vimieiro, we discovered that the drums were beating to arms along the line, and that the troops were forming, in order to meet some attack which appeared to be menaced.

A drizzling and soaking rain now began to fall, and we halted at a short distance before we reached the little stone bridge over the rivulet of Maciera, and which separated us from the Artillery park.

Upon this, I pointed out to Sir Hew the position near the two wind-mills, where Sir Arthur Wellesley and Sir Harry had, most probably, stationed themselves; and at the same time asked permission to ride on and announce his arrival; of which his Excellency at once approved.

On my seeking to meet with Sir Arthur, I soon discovered that, instead of a recommencement of hostilities, as every one had expected, the alarm which had extended to every part of the army had been caused by the advance of General Kellerman, who, instead of a small escort of fifty to sixty Cavalry, came up to within range of our advanced posts with a body of fifteen hundred Cavalry, before he displayed his white flag.

The rain continuing, I took shelter under some branches of a tree, in a garden, and overhanging the wall, exactly opposite the house occupied by Sir Arthur; and very soon afterwards the French General, with a handkerchief tied over his eyes, was led up on horseback to Sir Arthur's door, Colonel Walker being close by his side. The General now dismounted, and was conducted into the house.

This event, as may be readily expected, created a complete sensation throughout the army; and, after remaining more than an hour in expectation of the council of war being broken up, and that some kind of outline of the negociations might transpire, I quitted my post, and returned to the park, whence I observed several officers and parties of soldiers marching up from the sea-side, where they had just landed from England to reinforce the army.

The greater portion of the afternoon and after dinner was passed in conjectures as to the result of this conference; and I lay down for the night tired and worn out with expectation, for Kellerman was still at head quarters.

After remaining under arms until one hour after daylight on the 23rd, the army marched. I soon came up with General Fane, of the Light Brigade, by whose side I continued during some time, when, to my great surprise, a mounted officer, in the uniform of the 18th Hussars, at a round canter rode up from behind, and driving into an opening, about sufficient for half the width required for his horse, between Fane and myself, nearly pitched me over into a ditch, at the same time loudly expressing his particular satisfaction in meeting his old friend Fane, and shaking him by the hand. I could not resist staring at the Hussar, and not with a most pacific feeling;

but I was immediately introduced to Brigadier-General, the Honourable Charles Stewart, afterwards Marquis of Londonderry.

Having passed a small village, called Oz Cunhados, we arrived on some pine-clad hills, very much intersected by ravines, and here the army was ordered to halt and bivouac.

CHAPTER XV.

In making a sketch of the ground occupied by the army, I lose my way—A heavy storm—Alarmed again by the horses—A court-martial—Arrival of more troops—Major Fletcher supersedes me in the command—The whole of the army reviewed.

BEFORE my marquee was completely erected, I commenced making a general military sketch of the ground occupied by the army, and of as much of the surrounding country as I might find practicable in a limited time; and I also sent out the officers under my command, allotting to each a portion, to be filled up in detail, which would furnish the materials wherewith a very useful plan of our position might be put together in the shortest time possible.

I found the country difficult, and so covered with woods, that every part required to be gone over, as I could see but very short distances from any one spot; and, to my exceeding regret, dinner-time passed, and evening came on, long before I had completed my task.

As the sun went down, the sky became covered with black clouds, and threatened a storm from the South-West quarter; and, although some distant lightning flashed occasionally from almost every point of the compass, and that I felt exceedingly exhausted, having had no food since breakfast at three o'clock that morning, I persevered in my occupation, anxious to accomplish it that day; and I fully believed that, with proper exertion, I might do so before the closing of daylight.

Shortly afterwards, as it frequently happens in such weather, the sun having totally disappeared, the arch of dark clouds which had been slowly rising from the South-West, now made sudden and very rapid advances, without any perceptible wind, causing a degree of obscurity similar to that of night, and which the high and compact vault formed by the pine tops materially assisted and increased. I must at this time have been at some considerable distance from the army, and I now paused to reflect on the direction I ought to follow, in order to waste as little time as possible in rejoining my companions. Not a sound broke the dismal silence of this extreme solitude, but an occasional rattle of the woodpecker, or the cawing of a crow, as the latter in fear hastened away to hide from the approaching storm; and sometimes doubtful signs, like howlings of wolves, rose from the bottom of a distant valley, echoed from opposite and surrounding hills.

At length I moved on, as well as I could determine, towards the West; but long before I could extricate myself from this remote and very obscure part of the forest, extending along the borders of a grumbling rivulet, that descends one of the deep ravines into the wide planes below, I fancied I had totally lost my way. I, nevertheless, went on ascending at random, and I felt more indebted to accident than to any other cause for reaching my marquee by about ten o'clock, and upon which I had hit quite unexpectedly, from a quarter entirely opposite to the one in which I had expected to find it.

On entering the tent, I found it so entirely filled that there was not a spot left unoccupied where I could extend my wearied limbs: as to food, it would have been quite unreasonable to have enquired for any at that late hour, when all had finished their last meal, and when the dish was invariably cleared of the last morsel. I could not refrain from noticing the extreme selfishness of my visitors, who had, through my indulgence, been permitted to obtain a shelter under my humble roof, yet who had not had the gratitude to leave me any space, in order that I might participate in that shelter which exclusively belonged to me.

My temper was a little disturbed, and I well remember that I expressed my feelings somewhat strongly on this occasion, particularly on the want of common courtesy, and even of a proper degree of respect due to me as Commanding Officer, and which in this case seemed to prevail. To my observations all turned a deaf ear, and pretended to be sleeping very soundly; and, lest I might entertain any doubt as to that fact, several of them soon began to snore in a most exquisite style.

The darkness which overspread the sky was now almost perfect; but, with the aid of some bright flashes of lightning, I perceived a small spot, about the middle of the marquee, which seemed to be untenanted, and with much care, in order to avoid treading on any of the snorers, I managed to gain a footing on this space.

I now discovered that the vacant spot was unoccupied in consequence of being a natural bump in the ground, not very unlike the mounds formed over the graves of the departed in our burial-grounds, and which, no doubt, had caused it to be deserted. After some consideration, as to the best mode I could adopt, in order to keep myself from rolling off if I should lay myself down upon it, I went to the bag containing the tent pickets and mallets, always placed close to the door, and having driven four or five of these pickets into the ground in a straight line, along the edge of the long side of the mound, to keep me from falling off, I lay down, and found that I had succeeded in rendering this rejected position very habitable.

During all this time the lightning was augmenting in brilliancy, and the grumbling thunder had grown louder and louder, rolling on after every first burst, and rebounding from cloud to cloud, and from hill to hill, until again supplied by fresh explosions; so that no intermission was perceptible. Now, a gust of hurricane-like wind made the trees tremble and bend to their roots, and was quickly heard roaring down the ravines as it passed on over the black forest; and the death-like stillness which instantly succeeded was romantically awful, but of short duration, for the heavy drops of rain, mixed with scattered hailstones as large as musket-bullets, soon commenced beating such a *reveillé* on the tightly-strained canvas, which alone separated us from the contending elements, as announced that the storm was on us, and likely to be very severe.

All these preliminaries went on increasing, until the noise of the hail, the rain, the howling wind, and thunder grew to such a pitch as to be almost deafening; and it was now that the loud crashing of the falling trees created an additional and a very frightful source of anxiety to the whole army I may say; for it was not possible that a single individual could have remained plunged in sleep amidst such an uproar.

Before the expiration of five minutes from the commencement of the rain, I heard a general rising amongst the inmates of my mansion, when swearing and laughing was so profusely intermixed with semi-yelps, that for a moment I was greatly puzzled, and quite unable to guess at the reason which had suddenly created so much confusion.

I was not, however, left many seconds half breathless with suspense, when I understood that a perfect torrent had forced its way through the marquee, which had been most injudiciously pitched on sloping ground, without taking the ordinary precaution of forming a small ditch round the outside, and close to the foot of the walls.

Upon my mound, however, I lay on an

island, high and dry amidst the foaming stream, whilst my friends were dripping with water; for the rapid torrent had entered with a burst, as it overpowered the feeble and momentary resistance presented by the canvas walls, and had dashed in with such a volume at once, that in the twinkling of an eye, it had displaced every particle of air betwixt their skins and their shirts, and had commenced to wash their feet, sparing them the trouble of taking off their boots. All this had been accomplished, before they had been sufficiently roused to know distinctly what in reality had occurred, and what, under such pressing circumstances, was best to be done, in order to extricate themselves from the danger of being drowned.

Whilst I remained in security, occupying the rejected mound, I admit I was wicked enough to laugh heartily; and I very sincerely rejoiced at the thorough drenching which it was evident my company had suffered, and which, in my opinion, they had very justly merited.

My gratification was, however, of very short duration, for in the midst of this confusion, which, it might be supposed, could not have been augmented, I heard a general cry of "The wolves are coming in!" whilst others vehemently exclaimed, "For God's sake, keep out the horses!"

At the cry of "The wolves are coming in!" I jumped up, and stepping forward with my sword drawn, but raised as far as the roof would allow, not to hurt friends, and keeping my eyes fixed in the direction of the door, in an instant I observed that it was open, and I saw the red glaring eyes of excited animals, one rearing its head over the other, but which were too high to be those of wolves, and a succession of brilliant flashes of lightning clearly presented to view a drove of horses, in countless numbers, contending with each other for the earliest admission into the marquee.

Upon this discovery we thought that, by calling on the horses to retire, in the usual polite manner practised by grooms in addressing those faithful animals, they would have felt intimidated, and would have immediately desisted from further attempts at intrusion; but, however efficacious such language might be in ordinary cases, it clearly appeared that the extreme terror of the horses was such, that the more they became assured of the presence of human beings, the more tenacious they had become of remaining with us, as they seemed to fancy themselves somewhat protected by our society. All our efforts to drive away the horses were, therefore, quite fruitless, and all we could accomplish was to keep them from forcing their company upon us within the marquee.

Had these poor creatures been successful in their attempt, to which the severe beating of the heavy hailstones impelled them, they would, no doubt, have burst open the palace in every direction, upon which the roof would have fallen upon them; in which case, God only knows, under such circumstances, how many of us might have escaped with our lives; for it is certain, that none could have got off without severe injuries, as it cannot be doubted, that horses rendered wild with fear, and driven to desperation by the violence of a pelting hail, and terrified by the raging storm, would, on feeling themselves clasped all over by the clinging of the wet canvas, and the entangling cords, have commenced kicking at each other and at every thing; and as we should have been embraced in the same canvas, clasping us up tightly with the horses, as if all had been crammed into one immense straight waistcoat—who could have escaped under such pressing circumstances?

By midnight the storm having passed away, the horses were persuaded to remove to a distance, and I remounted my throne, the only dry spot left within many miles around us, excepting, perhaps, in some of the tents, of which there were only one to each corps.

The storm to which the army was thus exposed in the forest of Ramalhal, on the 23rd of August, 1808, was, indisputably, one of the severest ever experienced by troops *en bivouac*.

The position occupied by the army on the following morning after daylight presented a most novel appearance; from the lower branches of the trees were suspended in every direction great coats and spare clothing, in order to dry them, and giving to the *ensemble* very much the aspect of a rag fair.

In the course of this morning (24th of August), I was under the painful necessity of ordering a court-martial to assemble for the trial of one of the Royal Military Artificers, under my command, charged with marauding and committing sundry crimes unbecoming the character of a soldier, &c. The man was convicted, and sentenced to receive three hundred lashes in the usual manner, and, as usual, at the discretion of the commanding officer.

I approved of the proceedings and finding of the court; but having a great repugnance to the flogging system, and considering, moreover, how inconvenient, and, indeed, how almost impossible, it would have been to carry into effect such a punishment whilst the army was marching almost daily, I ordered that the culprit should receive twenty-five lashes only, leaving the remainder to hang over him *in terrorum*, and to be carried into effect in the event of my lenity failing to procure that salutary effect upon him which I confidently hoped it might. I have much gratification in recording that I was not disappointed, and that I was spared the affliction of being under the necessity of directing the execution of the remainder of the sentence, or of any part of it.

The heat of the sun having, in some degree, dried up the rain, we lost no time in completing the sketch of this position; and on returning to the army we found it augmented by several regiments, which, as often as the weather permitted, were landed from the fleet, lying on the coast; and it was very interesting to observe the frequent bursts of surprise, and exclamations of delight, manifested amongst all ranks as the numerous relations, friends and acquaintances most unexpectedly met each other. The hearty shaking of hands, the smiling and joyful faces, the rapid and anxious inquiries after other friends and relatives at home; the pleasure expressed by some, and the sudden changes to deep sorrow exhibited by a few, were scenes passing and occurring at every instant, and throughout every part of the bivouac.

The ground within my marquee had been so completely saturated with water, that I ordered it to be struck at an early hour, and towards evening the sun's rays had been so powerful that the surface at least was again tolerably dry. The marquee was therefore once more erected, the inequalities filled up and levelled with sods, and a proper ditch, a foot deep, was formed, entirely surrounding the walls.

My experience, gained in Canada, in the manner of making a field bed, had taught me that the tops of pine or spruce trees, when properly and regularly arranged on the ground, by making the delicate extremities cover the stems or stiff wood parts, compose a very comfortable bed; and which, moreover, possesses the advantage of being raised six or eight inches above the damp earth. I, therefore, ordered the whole bottom or floor of the marquee to be covered in that way; and on the following morning, the thanks of the whole of the inmates were unanimously voted me.

The greater part of this morning (25th)

was passed in sauntering about; some in search of muscatel grapes, others in groups debating on the probable results of the negociation, which it was known had been commenced with a view to a termination of hostilities; and I, myself, in rambling in every direction to procure some valuable additions to my sketch-book.

After dinner I joined a party, guided by one of our mess, to eat our dessert of muscatels in a vineyard which he had that morning discovered, within the limits necessarily prescribed to our walks; and we there not only found abundance of those exquisite grapes, but also some of the finest melons I ever tasted, which, of course, were growing entirely in the open fields.

Our army had now, by degrees, received considerable reinforcements; and, I believe, that the general officers arrived in far greater proportions than was due in regard of the soldiers. Lieutenant-General Sir John Moore, G.C.B., joined us, amongst the former.

Sir Hew Dalrymple very properly judged it expedient to review the whole army; but, instead of causing it to march past him, it was arranged that the line should be formed two deep, and that his Excellency would ride along its front, receiving the salutes as he passed.

Thirty thousand men, including the Portuguese under the command of General Freire, were drawn up in one line on the 26th of August; and a brilliant staff, amounting to sixty or seventy, at least, all well mounted, commenced riding along its front from the right, the regiments saluting and the bands playing as the Commander-in-Chief came up to the right of each regiment or brigade, and passing on at a full canter as frequently as the ground could permit.

It will be easily supposed that such a line, extending quite six miles in length, must have passed over a great variety of country, and enclosures formed of many high banks, with deep and wide ditches.

Now, as no pioneers had been ordered to clear the way, the staff had to make a sort of steeple-chase of it; and as some of our Generals were no amateurs, every ditch we came to in succession deprived us of the honour of one or two Generals, and necessarily of their personal staff officers; so Sir Harry Burrard, the heaviest of the number, was the first to give it up.

Thus, step by step, we thinned away; so that on reaching the left of the line, Sir Hew, Sir Arthur, and a few more, with some of their respective attendants, including myself, were all that could boast of having inspected the whole of this splendid line, composed of the flower of the British Isles; although many of them had not handled a musket more than six months; but when opposed to the French at Vimieiro, they had, at the points of their bayonets, extorted from those veterans in war, the highest encomiums for their steadiness, their discipline, and their valour.

I had not returned many minutes to the bivouac, when, to my extreme astonishment, I perceived an officer of Engineers at a distance coming up on foot, who was a stranger to our army, but was known by several of us at once to have just landed from England, and whose gait, on further observation, was familiar to me; in a few moments I held by the hand my very worthy and most excellent friend, Major Fletcher, whom I had left as second in command of the Royal Engineers, at Portsmouth, two years and a half before that time.

I surrendered my command to Fletcher, having held it exactly ten days since the battle of Roliça.

CHAPTER XVI.

Advance to Torres-Vedras—Procure a cloak—Dine with Fane—Wine in a wide dish—Having lost my right to a marquee, I sleep in a church-porch with Fane—Sketch of the ground—The Zizandra—Interesting dialogue stopped in the nick of time—Bivouac at Monte-de-Agraça—Proceed by the Pass of Bucellas to San-Antonio-de-Tojal—Sir Arthur retains the command of his troops as a Division—Captain Elphingstone comes to the army to take leave of us—His wound appears quite cured—On passage to England he brings up his three teeth—We are all displeased at being kept out in open air—Lawson and myself ride off into Lisbon, and arrive at the American hotel.

SOME cause, with which I am at present unacquainted, having diminished the means of transport with the army, it was thought, by issuing three days' rations of biscuit to the troops, a large quantity of the weight would be thus disposed of. Accordingly, prior to marching off on the 27th, the said quantity of biscuit was served out to the army, but the greater portion of it was left on the ground in small heaps, the men being unwilling to increase their loads. This, at the time, was regarded as a sort of rebellious conduct, but I never heard it had been followed by any further demonstration of insubordination.

Our day's march was short, and performed through a very picturesque country, part of which was thickly wooded; and at an early hour we entered the pass leading into the valley of Torres-Vedras.

On the hills extending right and left of this fine verdant flat valley, and at the Northern side, the army was bivouacked; and on the opposite side of which is the town, situated at the base of the old castle, on an insulated mount. In a very meandering course, flows a small rivulet, fordable at all parts, and over which, between us and the town, was a small stone bridge carrying the road between two rows of trees, and then immediately enters the town.

This bridge was now declared to be the utmost limit of our advanced posts : the town in front was neutral ground ; but with a written permission from the General of the Light Division, I had the good fortune to be allowed to go into town.

Notwithstanding the most rigid prohibition, I met at every corner, and saw in every shop, some of our officers, and even privates ; and here, for the first time, I met Lord Burghurst, attended by a Portuguese priest, whom he had hired to wait on him constantly, as a useful guide and convenient interpreter.

On this occasion my first object was to procure some kind of additional covering, and I had the extraordinary luck to secure the last ready-made cloak for sale in the town ; for everything was with avidity purchased, so that in less than two hours every article of provision, or of clothing, without exception, had been seized, and paid for at the price demanded.

I shall never forget the delight, amounting to a sort of pride, which I experienced on finding myself the proprietor of this notorious brown cloth cloak; and no one can duly appreciate the value of such an article, who has not experienced the suffering of lying in the open air, no matter how bleak the situation, during every change of wind, and alteration in the dryness or moisture of the atmosphere, in the rain or in the dew, without any kind of covering, excepting such as officers usually have on, during the summer season, in a warm climate.

My anticipation of the comfort I had now secured was so delightful in imagination, that I almost wished night would immediately commence, in order that I might have the inconceivable comfort of lying down well rolled up in my famously thick and long cloak, without feeling the dew from above, or the damp ground underneath me.

General Fane here invited me to dine with him; and as there was not a drop of wine in the canteens, Schwalbach was furnished with the necessary authority in writing, for passing the advanced guard on the bridge, and also with money for the purchase of wine.

The dinner had been ready during some time, but our purveyor was not in sight. I was sitting on the brow of the hill by the side of a windmill on the left of the road, as it enters the valley from the North, and with my telescope straining my sight to catch the first glimpse of friend Schwalbach on his return, when, after puzzling my head to find out the cause of his long delay, I, at length, caught sight of something advancing like a rifleman; but he had, as I then thought, a large Chinese hat on his head, instead of his military cap.

"This fellow," thought I, "greatly resembles Schwalbach in all matters excepting the strange covering of his head."

I called the General to look at him, who was equally unable to make out the cause of so novel a head-dress; Bringhurst and Mac Lean were as much perplexed, and we all continued to keep this man in sight until he actually came so near as to be sure he was in reality friend Schwalbach, who, instead of being the bearer of a keg, a stone bottle, a jar, a pot, a pitcher, or a basket of bottles, had on his head a brown earthenware deep dish, a yard wide or more, and, of course, only about half-full.

We were greatly diverted, and laughed most heartily as Schwalbach deposited on the ground this immense dish, whilst he was perspiring most violently, and declaring that he had never in his life been so fatigued by carrying any weight. He said, that to keep the dish level on his head and the wine from splashing out, had strained his movements so much, that nothing could equal it. The wine was most excellent, in our estimation, and we drank to the health of the rifleman.

By the arrival of Fletcher I had lost the benefit of the marquee shelter, and was again reduced to the open-air system. Consequently, during the daylight, I had kept a look-out for the best night quarters; and having espied a handsome church near the advanced post on the bridge, General Fane, his staff, and myself, resolved on taking possession of the portico, which in form somewhat resembled that of St. Martin's-in-the-Fields, in London, but of far less beauty.

In lying down, we agreed that the situation appeared to be so well ventilated, that it was quite unnecessary to leave any spaces betwixt us for that purpose, but that the close contact of our persons would procure us a few degrees of additional warmth, for the night air was very cold.

During the night the wind was strong from the South-West, with occasional showers; and as our portico faced towards the West, the elevated roof so far above our heads did not save us from a single drop of rain; we, therefore, came to the conclusion that it would not be difficult to find a more convenient situation on the following night, should the army not advance.

We all worked very industriously in making a good sketch of this position, for we remained on the ground at Torres-Vedras during three days.

After the first day we had free access to the town, when I availed myself of the opportunity to procure two or three Portuguese books, in order that I might attempt to make some progress in that language.

With this occupation, and my daily rambles in "*search of the picturesque*," to supply matter for the sketch-book, my time was profitably and agreeably employed.

I know not how it happened, but on the second day after our arrival near Torres-Vedras, I obtained a bell tent, which I pitched on the hill on the right-hand or Western side of the *debouché* of the pass, as it enters into the plain or valley; and having employed my servants in forming my favourite pine-top bed, I slept each night, wrapped up in my cloak of luxury, from the moment when I lay down, until roused by the bugle for morning parade.

The French army having retreated towards Lisbon, we advanced to the same extent, and after passing through the town of Torres-Vedras, we followed a road leading off towards the left, and along the greater part of the way the paved road was good; and passing under an aqueduct, where rich gardens with vineyards extend on both sides,. we, at length, began to ascend into a less cultivated country, and ultimately arrived on some very elevated ground called Monte-de-Agraça, where the division of the army I was with halted.

In conformity with my constant practice, as soon as the position of the troops had been arranged I lost no time in reconnoitring the same and surrounding country; and in so doing on this occasion, I instantly discovered that our advanced sentinels were separated from those of the French by a very narrow and unimportant rivulet, I believe named "The Zizandra."

Here, on following the line of demarcation betwixt the two armies, I had frequent occasion to notice the very curious dialogues which were passing between the sentinels of the contending armies; and one in particular, which made a deeper impression on my memory, may be sufficiently illustrative of the general run of those exchanges of compliments which were incessantly occurring.

On my turning a sharp bend in this gutter, for it deserved no better name, I heard some words in French, and some in English, which induced me to halt whilst unobserved by the parties, although within a few yards of them, when I caught the following very interesting conversation:

"I say, mounseer, how do you do? parlé vou france? I say, how is master Nap?"

Of all this the Frenchman did not understand one word, but he quickly replied: "*Que dis tu, mon sacré godam? combien te donne-ton par jour?*"

"What's that you say, you hungry frog?"

"*Ah*, you *f— béte!*" half turning his back upon Johnny.

"Where's your rod and hook, what's the use of bait without?"

"*Allons, Monsieur John Bull, veux-tu une miche?*" throwing to our friend across the ditch a large piece of bread, for which he had been rummaging in his haversack during several minutes, and when he had drawn it forth, I observed a small-toothed comb was half-buried into the corner, but which the Frenchman had immediately withdrawn, and had carelessly thrown back into his haversack. John Bull could not be out-done in liberality by mounseer, so down he stepped into the ditch, holding up his canteen, and calling out to the Frenchman:

"I say, come here, you're a good fellow; come down here, and take a drop of rum to old Georgy's health."

The Frenchman could not mistake Johnny's meaning, so down he went, and carefully drawing apart a pair of moustachios half-a-yard long, and wiping his mouth on the sleeve of his coat, beginning at the elbow and terminating with the tips of his fingers, he bowed gracefully, and, touching his cap, applied the canteen to his sucker, taking in a good swig of John's rum, which to a Frenchman is always a treat, but at that time was an article of the highest luxury. The Frenchman, smacking his lips, and unable to mark his gratitude in any other way, threw both his arms round John Bull's neck, and began kissing him with all the affection he would have shown to his own father.

John, at this, started back, tearing himself from the Frenchman's embrace; and, full of rage, he exclaimed, "Do you take me for a girl, or what sort of pranks would you be after?" and as he extricated his neck from the tight hold of his friend, fetched him a dry wipe across the face with the back of his hand, which well nigh floored him. By this time I had crept up close to these gentlemen, and perceiving that some very serious consequences were likely to result from this total ignorance of each other's intentions, I interposed, and being master of the French language, I succeeded in satisfying both parties that there did not exist the slightest cause for carrying this affair any further. The Frenchman was by far the most difficult to appease, and repeatedly exclaimed, "*Un soufflet ne se pardonne pas.*" He had received a slap on the face, an insult too gross to be easily repaired; he had therefore already drawn his sabre, and was vehemently and loudly calling on Johnny for that satisfaction which one gentleman has a right to demand of another.

From this bleak position I was unable to find any landscape worthy of being sketched. The views over the surrounding country are very extensive, but far from picturesque: there being no trees, nor even much brush-wood, we suffered greatly through the scarcity of fuel and the total absence of shelter, for the night, on that elevated spot, was severely cold;* and although the small rivulet in our front supplied us and our horses with water, yet it was neither clear nor abundant. It was therefore without regret that, after morning parade, I observed the troops march off and follow the high road towards Lisbon.

Accordingly, having descended from our elevated position, and passing on our left the small town of Bucellas, surrounded by the vineyards producing the wine named after it, we entered the grand and justly celebrated pass which extends from Bucellas to the open country on the south side of the considerable range of mountains that commence at the sea near Mafra, and continue Eastward without any break or opening until they arrive at this pass. The length of this defile is about four miles, and led to the open country, where we soon halted at a place called San Antonio de Tojal.

Being with Fane at the head of the advanced

corps, or light brigade, immediately on arriving at the southern extremity of the pass, I went off the road and placed myself in a position whence I could see about one and a half to two miles of the road through the pass.

The advance of the army along a winding, but nearly level road, carefully formed on the side of a very steep range of mountains, and which descended below into a rivulet rushing through a confined gully, at a great depth, produced a very imposing effect; whilst the numerous bands of music playing lively tunes, the colours waving in the breeze, and the prancing of gaily caparisoned horses composing the staff at the head of each brigade, presented a *coup-d'œil* highly interesting, and far beyond my powers of description.

On débouching from the pass, the troops spread out to the right and left, and were immediately ordered to halt, and form their respective bivouacs.

Here I received a marquee, and being only about nine miles from the capital, we procured many comforts and better provision than had been hitherto attainable.

I should perhaps have mentioned before now, that on advancing from Torres Vedras, whence there are three distinct roads leading to Lisbon, we had followed the one which passes to the Eastward of the others.

In saying *we*, I mean the troops that had gained the battles of this campaign; and although during the morning of the 21st of August, and following days, five or six officers, all senior to Sir Arthur Wellesley, had joined the army, without, however, bringing with them such reinforcements as might have provided each of them with a division, in consideration of Sir Arthur's achievements, the troops he had from the commencement led on to victory, or the greater part of them, were left together as Sir Arthur's division.

The other troops, which had subsequently joined, had, some of them, marched upon Lisbon by the central route, passing by the Cabeça de Monchique, which is the shortest, and the remainder by the Western line, through Mafra and Cintra.

Major Fletcher, being now the Commanding Engineer, had, of course, followed Sir Hew

MY MILITARY LIFE. 299

Dalrymple, the Commander-in-chief, so that from the period of our advance from Torres Vedras, I saw but little of him.

On the 2nd of September, a day or two after our arrival at San Antonio de Tojal, we were greatly surprised by a visit from Captain Elphingstone, who informed us that he was come from Lisbon to take leave of us, prior to his departure for England. He dined with us, and it caused a general astonishment on perceiving that his wound was externally quite cured, and that he was enabled to take his dinner without perceptible inconvenience.

A mark on his chin, rather on the left side, was visible, and resembled that which might have been made by pressure from a thimble. The skin was not only quite healed, but he had shaved over it, although Elphingstone's beard was one of the thickest and blackest that could be found. He informed us, that he had been shot whilst in the middle of the ploughed field at the foot of the ravine by which the 29th Regiment had stormed the heights of Columbeira (on the 17th of August), and was, as already told, at the time looking at the enemy through his telescope. The shock, Elphingstone stated, was so violent, that his arms flew out in a straight direction from his body as he fell to the ground from his little mule, and whence he was raised by Lieutenant Mulcaster, whom he had received from me as Adjutant.

Although the wound was doing so well that Elphingstone could eat with facility, the bone, although united, was not perfectly cured, and it was evident that a contraction of the lower jaw was taking place, in consequence of the vacancy caused by the ball in carrying away a piece of the bone with the three teeth mentioned on a former occasion, and which Elphingstone believed he had swallowed. Several years after this, Elphingstone, whom I had not seen since the day in question, informed me, that during his passage to England, whilst very sea-sick, he had brought up the said three teeth fastened together by the piece of jawbone, and which he showed me at Gravesend, in 1815, mounted in gold, and forming a brooch. Thus the teeth must have remained in Elphingstone's stomach during three weeks, at least.

Having remained several days at San Antonio de Tojal, in constant expectation of moving nearer to Lisbon, or into some of the forts in the vicinity of the capital, we began to grumble very much, and considered ourselves very ill-treated in being thus left in the open air, for very few of the officers were as yet under canvas; and this treatment we regarded as especially pointed at our division, since we understood that the others were all in good quarters, even those just arrived from Madeira under Major-General Beresford.

A few days after our arrival at this place, having taken an early breakfast, I mounted my horse without any premeditated plan, but merely with a view of taking a ride on the road leading towards Lisboa. I had not proceeded far, when I overtook Captain R. Lawson, of the Royal Artillery; and he also had no fixed object in mind.

After proceeding some distance, conversing on the chances we might have of being marched off into Spain without being first removed into Lisboa; it occurred to us that we should not be incurring much risk were we to ride on at once into the city, a place I had ever most ardently desired to see; and upon inquiring of a Portuguese gentleman whom we met, and who fortunately understood the French language, how far we then were from town, he replied that half an hour would take us there. " Not more than half an hour!" we both simultaneously exclaimed. This discovery settled the affair. " In half an hour!" said I to myself; " I am determined not to postpone to another day the gratification of a desire of such long standing."

Lawson also had never been at Lisboa, and as he offered no objection, off we started at a full trot, and almost immediately entered the suburbs. Onwards we went steering by the sun, as nearly as we were able, to the Southward, which we knew must lead us to the Tagus.

This was, of necessity, our only guide, for at this time we both spoke the Portuguese language so imperfectly, that we could neither have inquired our way, nor could we have understood an answer; and moreover, a far more important difficulty existed in our being totally unacquainted with the name of any particular spot or place in the city. Our object at that moment was confined to a ride through the principal streets. At first we totally failed, by keeping too much to the left, by which we became bewildered amongst the most wretched streets in Lisboa, extremely narrow and crooked, and half leg deep in the filthiest dirt for which that city is so celebrated. However, after many ups and downs along the steepest streets I ever saw frequented by horses, our reconnoissance was attended with better success; for by degrees we worked our way to the Praça-do-Comercio, and there, by inquiring of the French troops closely encamped and covering the immense square, we arrived at the American hotel, a dirty place enough, on the Caes-de-Sudré, the principal landing-place, but very pleasantly situated, overlooking the Tagus and its crowds of shipping.

CHAPTER XVII.

At the American hotel we meet other officers—We visit a coffee-house—French officers astonished at our appearance—We drink punch together—In attempting to go back to the hotel, we lose our way—Sleep on a stone seat in front of the hotel and return to camp—Lieutenant Wells, Royal Engineers, returns to us; his account of being made prisoner—The Duke of Abrantes gives a grand breakfast—Sir Arthur gives Junot a sharp cut—The General Officers subscribe for a piece of plate to be presented to Sir Arthur; and the Field Officers do the same.

We had been so long in finding our way, that on reaching the hotel it was nearly two o'clock, and on inquiring if we could have some dinner prepared, the waiter informed us there was an ordinary about to be served up, stairs, and that we should there meet with several English officers.

The information was most agreeable, for it exactly fitted the sharpened state of appetite which six hours' riding had not failed to excite; we, therefore, hastened to the diningroom, and soon joined Major Chichester Mc Donald, of the 82nd Regiment, and Major Henry Gomm, of the 6th Regiment.

I never enjoyed a dinner so much in my life. I had not had anything in the shape or form of a regular dinner since I had embarked at Gibraltar, on the 12th of May, nearly four months before; the fish, the vegetables, fruits and wines, were all, I thought, by far the best I had ever tasted.

After taking a moderate quantity of port wine, which I thought very superior in quality to any I had ever imbibed, we all sallied out together, without, I believe, any premeditated plan of operation. Having crossed diagonally the small square called the Caes-de-Sudré, and being about to turn the corner, which would have taken us along the street Do-Arzenal, we observed that the corner house was a coffee and ice house, and on looking into the windows it appeared to be well filled with French officers. "Let us go in," said one of us; "With all my heart," replied each of the others; and we found ourselves in the midst of those very men whom but two to three weeks before, we were fighting on the plains of Vimieiro.

Our appearance in the room, as may be well imagined, created a general sensation; all eyes were directed upon us full of inquiry; the most perfect silence prevailed. With as much nonchalance as I could master, I called out *garçon*, in as good French and as completely divested of foreign accent as if I were a native, and which excited the strongest symptoms of surprise on every countenance.

The waiter came as required, and I ordered *un bol de-ponche-aux-diable.* " *Morbleu !*" cried one ; " *Sacré-nom-d'ungueux !*" exclaimed another; " *Foutrrrrrr!*" vociferated a third ; and thus, every one to his own liking, expressed the degree of astonishment he felt, by some of those very common words, which, in reality, mean nothing, but which were incessantly current in the mouths of French grenadiers.

In an instant after we had been supplied with the punch, one of the French officers, a Voltigeur, quitted his seat very majestically, and came up to us, touching his cap in a soldier-like manner without bending his body, which we thought more soldier-like than officer-like, and addressed us in French; when having expressed in a very blunt and stiff manner the great satisfaction he felt at seeing us amongst them, and in which he felt assured every one of his brother officers then present participated, he anxiously inquired if I were not a native of France, adding at once that he supposed I might be one of the unfortunate individuals who had emigrated, in consequence of the great revolution, which had commenced about the year 1790; and I believe, that notwithstanding my most earnest protestations to the contrary, he retained some doubt as to the fact.

The example of this Light Infantry man was immediately followed by a Captain of Grenadiers, and then by several others, so that each of them having taken a glass of punch, our bowl was emptied in a moment; but, as these fellows were no spoonies, they ordered the next bowl, and in this way turn-about punch was ordered and disposed of, until we had all taken as much as we could conveniently carry away.

After recounting innumerable anecdotes of the most incredible escapes which they had all experienced in the late battles with us, and particularly adverting to the *machines-infernales*, a name they applied to the Shrapnells, or Spherical case, then a complete novelty; we contrived to separate and take leave of each other, each of us fully intending to tumble into bed with the least possible delay.

However, on sallying into the street from a room containing an atmosphere so impregnated with the fumes of spirits, that I am almost surprised we did not all blow up like the explosions so fatal in collieries, we turned to the right instead of turning to the left; a mistake not very difficult to be understood, nor very uncommon, considering that we had found the port wine so good at dinner, and the punch so much better when drinking to the healths of George the Third, Napoleon, Sir Arthur Wellesley, the Duke of Abrantes, and to all the French and English Field-Marshals.

We thus followed the Rua-do-Arsenal, which very soon brought us to the grand square called Praça-do-Commercio, the south side of which is bounded by the Tagus, and which was completely covered with French soldiers *en-bivouac*, and round which sentinels were planted at every four or five yards. Here we were challenged by every one of these sentinels as we passed along towards the Rua-Aurea, and the *qui-vives* were so incessant, that we went on constantly calling out *Officier-Anglais*, without keeping a very strict account, so as to be sure that our answers were as numerous, and not more so than the interrogations of the sentinels.

Major McDonald and Lawson having left us, Gomm (brother of Sir William) and myself rambled about during some time, unable to find our way to the American hotel, when, to our astonishment, we met some of the same French officers from whom we had separated at the coffee-house door; and having acquainted them with our dilemma, they very obligingly reconducted us back to the door of our hotel, although we had wandered from the place a mile at least; and on their wishing us a good night, recommended that we should force an entrance, unless the door were instantly opened.

The night was far advanced, the door was shut and barricaded for the night, and all our efforts to gain admittance having failed, we sat down on some stone seats nearly opposite the house, and thus slumbered away the remainder of the night.

By about six o'clock, to our great satisfaction, we were perfectly recovered from the overpowering effects of the punch, and rejoiced exceedingly at perceiving the windows of the American hotel reopening one after the other, and at length the door also was lazily thrown back.

We now swallowed a hearty breakfast, as hungry as wolves, when Lawson and myself mounted our horses, and by nine o'clock had returned to San-Antonio-de-Tojal.

One of the first effects of the convention of

Cintra, which had just been concluded, was to set at liberty all the officers and soldiers who had been made prisoners by the French during that campaign. It was, therefore, through this event that in the course of an hour after we had returned to Tojal, we were agreeably surprised by a visit from Lieutenant Wells, of the Royal Engineers, who had been made a prisoner on the 21st of August.

Wells was mounted on a good horse, which I believe he had purchased from one of Junot's Aides-de-camp, and in the course of the day he passed at Tojal, he gave us the most interesting account of his capture and consequences. He stated that during the battle of Vimieiro, Major-General Acland, observing some forward movement made by the Portuguese Cavalry, which he considered to be too much in advance, he directed him (Wells) to order them to fall back; upon this, Wells, whose sight was not very good, inquired of the General in what direction he should find the Portuguese Cavalry, and was informed, in reply, they were not within view from the spot they were on, yet he would find them just beyond some rising ground close by, and to which the General pointed. Wells accordingly started off on his pony, by no means a first-rate steed; and having no saddle, he had been obliged to content himself with a pad or pack-saddle, without stirrups, and thus proceeded in search of the Portuguese Cavalry, with as little delay as the above-named circumstances would permit. He ascended and descended, not only the first rising ground, beyond which he was instructed the object of his research would be found, but he went on over one or two more pieces of ground much resembling the first, when at length he espied a body of Cavalry. Before starting he had not been informed of any of the details of the style, colours, or general appearance of the Portuguese, and as those now before him were decidedly not English, they necessarily were the Portuguese, and as they had been represented as advancing, and that by far too forward, Wells could not be surprised at having found them at such a distance in advance before he could deliver General Acland's orders. In order to waste not a moment, he pressed on his pony, and riding straight up to the officer commanding the Cavalry, in the best French language he could collect, for he was totally ignorant of the Portuguese, he delivered a faithful translation of the order. The Cavalry officer, who had advanced a few yards to receive this communication, a piece of courtesy Wells could not fail to appreciate, replied by *"plait-il,"* and *"que dites vous, Monsieur ? Le Général demand si nous voulons nous rendre ;"* which he pronounced in very good French, but with an air of extreme surprise.

Upon which, Wells repeated the order very gravely, and said, *" Le Général vous ordonne de vous retirer, Monsieur."*

"What General?" exclaimed the Cavalry officer.

"General Acland, sir."

"But to whom was that order addressed?" was quickly demanded.

"To the Portuguese Cavalry," Wells as promptly replied.

" Ma fois, voilà que est plaisant," laughing most heartily, the officer said, and taking Wells by the arm ; "come along then, you are my prisoner."

It is not difficult to understand that the Cavalry to whom Wells had delivered the order were the French. On this, one of the soldiers rushed at Wells and snatched away his sword. Thus made a prisoner, Wells was sent off to Junot, who desired that he should be conducted to the rear, where he would find many of his *camarades*. Upon this, Wells grumbled, and manifested some disapprobation, which Junot observed, and inquired what he might have to complain of; when Lieutenant Wells explained he had seen the commencement of the battle, and thought it very vexatious he should not see the end of it. Junot was pleased at the gallant feeling so oddly displayed, and addressing Wells, said, " Well, sir, give me your word of honour you will not leave me, nor attempt to escape, and you may remain with me." The pledge was gladly given, and Wells remained with the French Commander-in-Chief, and thus obtained the summit of his wishes. The French army having returned to Lisbon, whither our friend Wells had also been removed, the Duke of Abrantes took much notice of him, and invited him to his table, when on one occasion, Wells asked Junot why he had attacked the English army at Vimiciro? The question might as well have been omitted, since Junot had experienced a signal defeat on that occasion; yet, without manifesting any offence at being thus placed on his defence by so young an officer, he replied, " *C' est, mon cher, parceque j'aime mieux donner l'assaut que d'étre attaqué.*" Thus very adroitly towards himself, and in a very kind way towards Wells, getting rid of a question difficult to be otherwise dealt with.

In the course of a few days after our arrival at San-Antonio-de-Tojal, I had the honour of dining with Sir Arthur Wellesley for the first time, and I thought his quarters very good. All I remember of this event is, that the party was small, that Sir Arthur wore an air of good spirits, was entertaining, talked freely with every one, asked me to drink wine with him in a familiar manner, and that I passed a very agreeable afternoon.

Just about the same time the Duke of Abrantes gave a grand public breakfast at Lisbon, to which the generals and officers of their respective staffs were invited, and at which I was present, General Spencer taking me with him as attached to his staff.

In the course of the conversation that passed betwixt Sir Arthur Wellesley and the French Commander-in-Chief during the breakfast in question, the Duke of Abrantes observed to Sir Arthur, that on the 21st he had narrowly escaped being made a prisoner by one of our Dragoons who had closely pursued him, and upon which he had said that he would have been a grand prize to the man, for he was well worth one thousand guineas on that occasion.

Junot then went on relating that his orders were all set in brilliants, his sword and pistols mounted in gold, and of great value; an elegant gold repeater set round with jewels; rich gold chain, seals, and precious stones; gold snuff box with brilliants; his epaulettes, gold spurs, saddle, bridle, saddle cloth, housings, all laced and embroidered; and, in short, his purse, his sash, his horse, &c., &c., these were worth, at least, one thousand guineas; and then proceeded with considerable self-satisfaction, and raising his voice: "*Ma foi, Sire Artare,* (Sir Arthur), *je valais bien mille guinées, ce jour là, car j'étois en mon plus-beau! jour de bataille etant* TOUJOURS;" but hastily checking his bombast, went on, "*C'est à dire, ordinairement jour de fête,*" dropping his voice.

Upon which Sir Arthur, who had not altered a single muscle of his face whilst he attended to Junot's vanity, replied, or rather cut in with, "*Oui, quelque fois,*" preserving the utmost gravity, without looking to the right or left.

Soon after this event, the superseding of Sir Arthur Wellesley in the chief command of the British army then in Portugal, had produced a strong feeling of regret and disapprobation; he was regarded by those who had served under his command from the commencement of the campaign as having been shamefully treated.

The high respect, publicly and privately, entertained towards his Excellency had now been roused, and was immediately manifested by a subscription amongst the field officers and officers commanding corps, to collect a sufficient fund for presenting a piece of plate to Sir Arthur Wellesley, as a testimony of that sincere esteem and high respect with which his talents and conduct had so justly inspired them.

The whole of the preliminary arrangements for carrying into effect this determination had been completed without my knowledge, which I attributed to no want of proper feeling towards me personally, but simply because I was not at that time a field officer; and it was not before I had fully explained my right, as having commanded the corps of Royal Engineers during a great portion of the battle of Roliça, and during the whole of the battle of Vimieiro, that I was permitted to participate in the honour of subscribing my quota.

Colonel Kemis, commanding the 40th Regiment, as the Senior Field Officer with Sir Arthur Wellesley's army, was charged with conveying to His Excellency a respectful address from the individuals above alluded to, and which was carried into effect about the 18th of September.

The general officers who, in like manner,

had served during the campaign, also presented a piece of plate to the late Commander-in-Chief, but I have never had an opportunity of seeing either of these testimonials: they were necessarily on a small scale, but were as elegant and as well designed as the limited funds could procure.

From this period the troops that had served under Sir Arthur Wellesley, in the various engagements we had had with the enemy, were kept in the open fields very scantily supplied with tents, and at the distance of nine to twelve miles on the north side of Lisbon, whilst all the newly-arrived reinforcements were, on landing, comfortably quartered in Lisbon and its dependencies. This partiality excited some strong feelings of dissatisfaction, and I believe that the greater portion, if not the whole of the former, were marched off into Spain from their encampments and bivouacs, extending from San Antonio de Tojal to Cintra, without having been marched into Lisbon.

Here properly ends the first campaign of the Peninsular War, as regards Portugal. I shall therefore close this Second Part of my

Adventures and Recollections, reserving the many highly and interesting events connected with the embarcation of Junot's army and sequel for the commencement of the Third Part, which I shall endeavour to prepare without delay.

THE END.

www.ingramcontent.com/pod-product-compliance
Lightning Source LLC
Chambersburg PA
CBHW060832190426
43197CB00039B/2558

of Christ should be at the center of any message that endeavors to bring about justice in a society.

Along with justice, love should be seen in the relationship with others in the life of a covenant person. Justice and love cannot be separated in a covenant life. This love is not just any love, but is the love comes from the sacrificial love of Christ. This love gives, perseveres and sacrifices in the relationship with others. A covenant person is a person of action. Justice and love mean nothing without an action. A covenant person lives to love others and to make a community a just society.

Bibliography

Bonar, A. Andrew. *Memoir and Remains of the Rev. Robert Murray M'Cheyne*. Edinburgh: Oliphant, Anderson & Ferrier, 1894.

Calvin, John. *Institutes of the Christian Religion*. Translated by Ford Lewis Battles. Philadelphia: The Westminster, 1960.

Luther, Martin. *Works of Martin Luther*. Philadelphia: Holman, 1915.

Wakefield, Gordon Stevens. *Puritan Devotion*. Eugene, OR: Wipf & Stock, 2015.

Warfield, B. B. *Biblical and Theological Studies*. Philadelphia: Presbyterian and Reformed, 1968.

www.ingramcontent.com/pod-product-compliance
Lightning Source LLC
Chambersburg PA
CBHW050827160426
43192CB00010B/1931